Berlitz
Bruges and Ghent

Text by Jack Messenger and Brigitte Lee
Revised by George McDonald
Edited by Jeffery Pike
Principal photographer: Chris Coe
Managing Editor: Tony Halliday

Berlitz® POCKET GUIDE

Bruges and Ghent

Fifth Edition 2003 (updated 2004)

PHOTOGRAPHY BY
Pete Bennett 26, 40, 49, 56, 69, 73, 75, 79, 81, 96, 97; Chris Coe 6, 9, 11, 13, 19, 24, 27, 29, 35, 38, 41, 51, 55, 61, 64, 77, 86, 89, 90, 95, 99; Jerry Dennis 22, 30, 32, 34, 39, 44, 85, 87, 91, 93; Tony Halliday 16, 31, 37, 43, 46, 47, 50, 82; Georgie Scott 59, 63, 66, 67, 71, 74
Cover picture: Chris Coe

CONTACTING THE EDITORS
Every effort has been made to provide accurate information in this publication, but changes are inevitable. The publisher cannot be responsible for any resulting loss, inconvenience or injury. We would appreciate it if readers would call our attention to any errors or outdated information by contacting Berlitz Publishing, PO Box 7910, London SE1 1WE, England. Fax: (44) 20 7403 0290; e-mail: berlitz@apaguide.co.uk www.berlitzpublishing.com

The 12th-century island fortress of Gravensteen, stands in the heart of Ghent (page 67)

Onze-Lieve-Vrouwekerk, one of Bruges' oldest and finest churches is a warehouse of religious artworks and treasures (page 35)

Cruising round the canals is a relaxing way to enjoy the historic sights of Bruges and Ghent (page 7)

TOP TEN ATTRACTIONS

Bruges' Groeninge Museum contains works by the Flemish Primitives (page 32)

▼

◄ Dating from the height of Bruges' prosperity, the mighty 13th-century bell-tower looms over the city (page 25)

The Basilica of the Holy Blood stands guard over the holiest relic in Bruges (page 28) ►

Visit Ghent's Fine Arts Museum to see masterpieces such as Pieter Brueghel's *Peasant Wedding* (page 74) **▼**

►

The Gothic splendour of Ghent's principle church, Sint-Baafskathedraal (page 58)

The gilded Gothic Hall of the Stadhuis in Bruges (page 26)

►

Laarne Castle, east of Ghent, is one of the best-preserved moated fortresses in Belgium (page 78)

►

CONTENTS

Fact Sheets

BRUGES, GHENT AND THE BELGIANS

The land that is now Belgium has been coveted and fought over for thousands of years. The modern visitor can still catch the faint echo of all the armies that have battled and died on the soil of Flanders. Today, the nation that once was criss-crossed by foreign forces is traversed by millions of visitors – most of them on their way to holidays elsewhere in Europe. More and more travellers, however, are learning the secrets of Belgium, having discovered for themselves two of the country's greatest treasures – Bruges and Ghent.

The histories of these two cities are everywhere written in their streets and buildings, in their art and their culture. Bruges, in particular, is justifiably famous for its sheer beauty. Ghent contains areas of great historical as well as artistic interest, but also has the feel of a vibrant town with plenty of other things on its mind. Then there's the compact geography of the two cities, which means that visitors can explore with ease on foot, by bike, and even by water.

> There is no need for a car in either Bruges or Ghent: the canal-side roads and paths make for excellent walking and cycling.

Water forms an important part of the landscape and economy of Ghent and Bruges. Canals link the two cities to one another, as well as to the coast and important industrial centres. A leisurely cruise along the canals in either city is an experience not to be missed, and one of the best ways of viewing the wonderful cityscapes.

It is, of course, people that constitute a city: there are about 120,000 in Bruges and around 230,000 in Ghent. Most of the

Canalside buildings along the Langerei in Bruges

population is Roman Catholic, and the virtues of community cohesion in work and play make up much of what it is to be Belgian. Tradition and family life are important, and people take their work and their pleasures seriously – which explains why the country produces over 450 different beers.

Something else that figures prominently in Belgium is the museum. The Belgians, at least in their civic life, have a passion for collecting and recording; Bruges and Ghent share in this national characteristic, with some superb museums and galleries. They also have a rich calendar of events *(see page 92)*, including Bruges' spectacular Procession of the Holy Blood and the Ghent Flower Festival.

Eating and drinking in Belgium are mostly hearty events and form an important part of life. Belgian cuisine is justly famous throughout the world, both for its quality and its quantity (you'll never go hungry in Belgium), and there are plenty of fine restaurants in Bruges and Ghent. An intrinsic part of everyday eating is the Belgian french fry *(frite)*, which is available everywhere. Equally ubiquitous are the exquisite Belgian chocolates you will see in mouth-watering shop displays.

The Belgians have a strong sense of pride in their achievements and their history. Each town and city – Bruges and

---

Not Far Away

Belgium is a compact country (less than 325 km/200 miles across at its widest point), so nowhere is very far from anywhere else. Most of the other places of interest listed in this guide are within a few miles of Bruges or Ghent, themselves connected by a half-hour train journey. Those places farther away are easily accessible, thanks to the country's superb railways – in 1835 Belgium ran the first train in continental Europe.

Canal tours, available in both cities, are a relaxed form of sightseeing

Ghent in particular – have had distinctive roles in the development of the area. Before the foundation of the Belgian state in 1830, they were virtually autonomous city-states. Nationhood itself is a fiercely debated issue in Belgium. Both Bruges and Ghent are in Flanders, where the official language is Flemish (Dutch with a different accent). But a large part of the country is inhabited by French-speaking Walloons (there is also a small area of mainly German-speaking inhabitants). In fact, the residents of these two cities nearly all speak English and French, as well as Flemish.

Bruges and Ghent also take their visitors seriously. Tourist offices are friendly and informative, and in cafés, bars and hotels you will be served courteously, with patience and good humour. Whether you are staying for a weekend or using the two cities as bases for a longer tour, Bruges and Ghent will reward you with beauty, fascinating history and a warm welcome.

A BRIEF HISTORY

The nation of Belgium only came into being in 1830, but both Bruges and Ghent can lay claim to a very long and distinguished history. The story of the region begins with the Belgae, a Celtic tribe who lived there from Neolithic times. In the first of many occupations throughout the centuries, the Belgae were conquered in 54BC by the Romans under Julius Caesar. His account of the conquest of Gaul, as it was known, is recorded in his *Gallic Wars*. The small settlement that was to become Ghent dates from around this time.

The Kingdom of the Franks

With the decay of their empire early in the 5th century, the Romans withdrew from Gaul, much of which succumbed to the Franks, who had been settling in the region for the previous two centuries. They founded their Merovingian kingdom around Tournai in the south, while to the north and east the region was divided between Franks, Frisians and Saxons.

The conversion to Christianity of the Frankish King Clovis in 498 led to a gradual northward spread of the new faith, until the whole region became Christian – although the city of Ghent was one of the last bastions of paganism in Gaul. The settlement started to develop in the 7th century when St. Amandus founded two abbeys here, but not before a few devout Ghent pagans had thrown the missionary into the River Scheldt.

The first recorded mention of Bruges dates from the 8th century AD, though little is known about the town's origins, except that the name possibly comes from the Vikings.

In 768, the Frankish King Charlemagne established a unified kingdom. By military and diplomatic means he went on to found a European empire, culminating in his coronation by the Pope in 800 as Emperor of the West. On Charlemagne's death in 814, the empire passed to his son Louis, and on Louis' death in 840 was divided between his three sons. The division left a narrow strip of Europe, including the Low Countries (Belgium, Luxembourg and the Netherlands), sandwiched between French- and German-speaking nations.

The Golden Age of Bruges and Ghent

The area came under the nominal rule of a succession of German and French kings, but real power was in the hands of local nobles, who tried their best to weaken the hold over them by the French and German feudal kingdoms. Some of these lords were more wealthy than their rulers and negotiated charters of autonomous rights for towns in exchange for taxes and military assistance.

Gravensteen Castle – built in the 9th century, expanded in the 11th

Baldwin I (known menacingly as Iron Arm) built a castle at Bruges in the 9th century, and from there pursued a fierce expansionist policy to establish the county of Flanders. The first castle of Gravensteen in Ghent was built in the 9th century. In the 11th, the succession for Flanders passed to Robert the Frisian, who made Bruges his capital.

Despite the ongoing power struggles, the cloth towns of Flanders flourished in the 12th and 13th centuries. Ghent became the largest town in Western Europe, while Bruges had a population as large as that of medieval London, trading with the Orient, the Middle East and the rest of Europe.

International banks made Bruges their headquarters, foreign embassies located there, and the first stock exchange in Europe was founded in the city. Wool was vital to the economy: Bruges, Ghent and Ypres (Ieper) all prospered from the export of their manufactured cloth, and depended for raw material on imported wool from England. Bruges monopolised the trade in wool and, as a result, came to trade with the Hanseatic League, a powerful economic alliance of trading towns in northern Europe. The prosperity of the city reached a peak early in the 14th century.

> During what became known as the 'Joyful Entry' into Bruges in 1301, Queen Joan of Navarre marvelled at the rich apparel of the citizens: 'I thought I was the only queen, but there are hundreds more around me!'

But tension grew between the merchants who had every reason for keeping in with the King of England (because he controlled the supply of wool) and their lords, who usually sided with the French king. In the 13th and 14th centuries, the cloth towns of Flanders were the scene of frequent hostilities.

The most famous conflict became known as the 'Bruges Matins'. The French king, Philip the Fair, had invaded Flanders and appointed a governor whose taxation and suppression of the powerful guilds of Bruges were so severe that on the night of 17–18 May 1302 the city revolted, led by Pieter de Coninck and Jan Breydel. The resentful rebels killed everyone they thought to be French. In the same year the French were also defeated by the Flemish, at the Battle of the Golden Spurs near Kortrijk (Courtrai).

Shortly afterwards, Ghent was a centre of further rebellion. The city had been ruled since the late 10th century by a council who followed the wishes of the French monarchy. This incensed the independently minded guilds, and in 1337 a wool merchant named Jacob van Artevelde led the people of the city and other Flemish towns in revolt. He ruled Ghent as dictator until his murder in 1345.

In 1384 the region became part of the Burgundian realm. Duke Philip the Good of Burgundy became the Count of Flanders in 1419 and ushered in a new kind of

Jacob van Artevelde, rebel leader and dictator of Ghent

rule. He administered his possessions in Burgundy from Bruges, and he was the patron of a variety of artists, including Jan van Eyck and Hans Memling; the court became renowned for its splendour. In 1429 Philip received his fiancée, Isabella of Portugal, in Bruges – the cause for a celebration of sumptuous ostentation.

Ghent also came under Burgundian control, but the people of the city objected to the constant attempts of the French to suppress its guilds. In July 1453, thousands of Ghent citizens were killed in the Battle of Gavère, and city dignitaries had to beg for mercy. Charles the Bold, Philip's successor, and his bride Margaret of York enjoyed a lavish wedding in

Charles the Bold of Burgundy

Bruges when, it was said, the fountains spouted Burgundian wine. However, the splendour of Charles's reign did not last, and his death precipitated another French invasion of the south of the Low Countries. The people of Flanders took the opportunity to kidnap Charles's daughter Mary, forcing her in a charter to renew their civic rights (curtailed by Philip) before they would help fight the French.

The Habsburgs

Maximilian of Austria married Mary and assumed full control of the region immediately after Mary's death in 1482. The era of the powerful Habsburgs had begun. The burghers of Bruges still had the nerve to incarcerate Maximilian himself briefly in 1488, exacting further promises to acknowledge their rights, but Maximilian reneged on these as soon as he was released. His grandson Charles V, born in Ghent in 1500, continued a policy of favouring Antwerp rather than the cloth towns of Flanders – despite Bruges' reception of him amid great pomp and splendour in 1520. Charles' policy accelerated the economic decline of Bruges and Ghent; as well as their own mutual antagonism, they now had to contend with stiff competition from the cloth manufacturers in England. Bruges' death knell came when the River Zwin silted up, cutting off the town from the sea and ending its international trade; it did not awake from its economic slumber until the 19th century.

The Reformation

The movement we call the Reformation was bound to have strong appeal for the merchants and people of Flanders. It stressed the rights of individuals to read and interpret the Word of God for themselves, thanks to the invention of the printing press, and questioned the clergy's power to promulgate a world view controlled by the State and Church in alliance. With the emergence of Luther and Calvin, pressure for reform turned into outright revolt, leading to the establishment of alternative churches. Protestantism was born.

The Low Countries were particularly receptive to new ideas, as rich merchants chafed against the strictures of a rigidly hierarchical social system, while the artisanal guilds had always resented any royal authority.

Charles V's abdication in 1555 meant that the Low Countries passed on to his Catholic son, Philip II of Spain, and bloody conflict ensued. Philip and his sister Margaret harshly repressed Protestantism and tried to reinstate the authority of the Catholic Church. The 1565 harvest failure caused widespread famine and led to the Iconoclastic Fury, when workers ran riot among the Catholic churches, sacking and destroying everything. Frightened for their own positions,

Roped In

Although Ghent was the city of his birth, Emperor Charles V treated its citizens mercilessly in the 1530s when they launched a public protest against heavy taxation and a collapsing economy. He had the ring-leaders executed and forced the city's dignitaries to appear before him on their knees, bareheaded, each with a noose around his neck, and to beg him for mercy. To this day, the annual procession of the *Stropendragers* (Noose Bearers) recalls the humiliation that Charles forced upon the city.

the nobility sided with Margaret and Philip. In 1567 Philip sent an army to the Low Countries. The 'Pacification of Ghent', signed in the city in 1576, instated a short-lived period of peace and freedom of worship.

A subsequent war between the Spanish and the Dutch Protestants, led by William the Silent, resulted in the Low Countries being partitioned in 1579, with the Protestant north ultimately gaining independence and the Catholic south siding with the Spanish. This partition corresponds more or less to today's border between Belgium and the Netherlands.

War of the Spanish Succession

The Habsburg dynasty in Spain ended in 1700 when Charles II died without an heir. He had specified that Philip V of Anjou should succeed him, but the Habsburg Leopold II of Austria had other ideas. He did not like the thought of the grandson of the king of France ruling Spain, thus uniting the two kingdoms under one dynasty. He was prepared to fight for this belief and the resulting war lasted from 1701 to 1714.

Bruges' history is told in murals in the Stadhuis (Town Hall)

The treaty that ended the war signed over the Spanish Netherlands and Belgium to Austrian rule. They remained in Austrian hands under Archduchess Maria Theresa, and Belgium prospered through an arrangement whereby its trade was subsidised by Austria.

In 1780, Maria Theresa was succeeded by her son Joseph II. Although he fancied himself as a radical ruler and did institute several enlightened, secularising reforms, his lack of consultation and his 'top-down' approach to change created widespread resentment. Sporadic rebellions occurred from 1788, and in 1790 the 'United States of Belgium' was proclaimed, winning recognition from Britain and the Netherlands. The fledgling nation was defeated a year later by the forces of the new Austrian Emperor, Leopold II.

> It was during the reign of Maria Theresa that architecture, lace-making and art flourished, and Ghent's economic revival began with the establishment of the cotton industry. The distribution of all this new wealth was limited mainly to the aristocracy and the merchants, while the majority of the population barely managed to scrape a living.

French Invasion and Independence

Despite having received military assistance from a Belgian contingent against the Austrians in 1792, the army of revolutionary France invaded Belgium and the Netherlands two years later and occupied the annexed countries for the next 20 years – though not without some benefit to Belgium. The country was divided into a number of *départements* along French lines; important and unjust aspects of Church, State, and taxation were reformed or abolished. There was also rapid subsidised industrialisation, with France being the main market for Belgian manufactured goods.

Yet no country likes to be controlled by another. Rebellions broke out from 1798 onwards. Following the final defeat of Napoleon at the Battle of Waterloo in 1815, the Congress of Vienna perpetuated Belgium's subjugation by giving control of the country to the Dutch House of Orange. It was not until the revolution in 1830 that an autonomous free Belgian state was finally created. In 1831, the London Conference recognised the independence of Belgium and established it as a constitutional monarchy. Leopold I was awarded the crown.

Armageddon – Twice

Throughout the 19th century, Belgium modernised, immersing itself in the Industrial Revolution. Slowly, Bruges was being rediscovered by British travellers on their way to see the site of the Battle of Waterloo. Ghent revived, becoming a major economic centre. Yet tensions between the different linguistic groups within the new country became more obvious as persistent social difficulties failed to be resolved.

> In the mid-19th century, living conditions for working people were often appalling, aggravated by a dreadful famine in Flanders from 1845 to 1848. When Bruges became the capital of Flanders almost half the population was dependent on charity.

In need of a scapegoat, the predominantly Flemish-speaking (and increasingly prosperous) north agitated increasingly for independence from the (French-speaking) Walloon south. Instead of attending to the problems of his country, the new king of Belgium, Leopold II (1865–1909) devoted most of his time to personal interests, including a private colony in the Belgian Congo. Albert I, his nephew, succeeded him in 1909.

During Albert's reign, World War I gripped Belgium for four years. In 1914, the German army invaded, despite the country's neutrality, forcing the king to remove to a narrow remaining strip of unoccupied Belgium. His resistance to the invaders gained him international renown as the 'Soldier King'.

The northern front of the war extended roughly diagonally across the country, with the most infamous – and bloodiest –

of battles taking place around Ypres (Ieper) in southern Flanders. The ultimate defeat of Germany won Belgium considerable reparations and some new territory.

It might have been expected that the experience of war would have drawn the Belgian nation together, especially when King Albert proclaimed a series of reforms meant to improve equality between the Flemish and the Walloons. But as fascism was already working its way through both communities, they grew more antagonistic. In 1940, the Nazi German army marched into Belgium, occupying it in just three weeks (Bruges and Ghent suffered little damage, though the former's new canal had to be repaired extensively).

The Menin Gate in Ypres (Ieper) pays tribute to the war dead

A resistance movement formed from around 1941, including an underground network to protect Belgium's Jews. However, the behaviour of the king, Leopold III, who was eager to accommodate the invaders, caused much controversy after the war as Belgium sought to rebuild itself.

In 1950, the people voted by a narrow margin to ask the king home from exile, but Leopold decided to abdicate in favour of his son, Baudouin I.

Regionalisation

After forming Benelux, an economic union with the Netherlands and Luxembourg, Belgium went on to join the European Economic Community in 1957, with Brussels the seat of the organisation. Though this has ensured that Belgium is internationally recognised as the home of European bureaucracy, it has nevertheless retained its own distinct national character.

The country finally divested itself of the Belgian Congo (now the Democratic Republic of Congo) in 1960. Internal political events since the end of World War II have been dominated by the continuing friction between the Flemish and Walloons. In 1977, three federal regions were established – Wallonia, Flanders and Brussels – in the hope that greater self-determination would ease the tensions between the groups.

In 1989, regional governments were created, each with responsibility for all policy except matters concerning social security, defence and foreign affairs. A new Belgian constitution was adopted in 1994, establishing Belgium as a federal state.

The Procession of the Holy Blood in Bruges dates from medieval times

In practice, the universal courtesy of Belgians means that visitors today will see very little sign of inter-community tension. Bruges' ambitious restoration of its medieval centre attracts tourists from all over the world, and interest can only grow stronger following the city's high-profile year as European City of Culture in 2002. Similarly, Ghent is undertaking an intensive restoration programme in a move to attract a growing number of visitors and ensure its continued prosperity.

Historical Landmarks

58–51BC Roman conquest of Gaul, including present-day Belgium.

AD498 Conversion to Christianity of Frankish King Clovis.

700s Foundation of Ghent abbeys; first mention of Bruges.

768 Charlemagne's unified kingdom is established.

800s Castle built at Bruges.

814 Death of Charlemagne and division of empire.

864 Baldwin becomes first Count of Flanders.

1302 Bruges Matins and Battle of the Golden Spurs.

1337 Revolt of Ghent against French rule.

1384 Flanders becomes part of Burgundian kingdom.

1419 Philip the Good of Burgundy made Count of Flanders.

1453 Battle of Gavère. Burgundians defeat Ghent rebels.

1482 Habsburg reign begins with Maximilian of Austria.

1555 Charles V abdicates; Philip II succeeds.

1567–79 Religious wars in the southern Low Countries.

1701–14 War of the Spanish Succession.

1780 Maria Theresa dies; Joseph II accedes.

1790 Proclamation of United States of Belgium.

1794 French invade and occupy country for 20 years.

1815 Napoleon defeated, Waterloo; Congress of Vienna.

1830 Belgian revolution and independence.

1914–18 World War I; Germans invade neutral Belgium.

1940 Nazi Germany occupies Belgium during World War II.

1948 Benelux formed, with Belgium as member.

1949 Belgium joins NATO.

1957 Belgium becomes founding member of EEC.

1977 Establishment of three federal regions.

1989 Regional governments created.

1993 Albert II becomes king.

1994 New Constitution adopted, establishing Belgium as a federal state.

2002 Bruges is made European City of Culture. The Concertgebouw concert and opera hall opens in the city.

WHERE TO GO IN BRUGES

Bruges is made for walking: it is very compact, with attractions clearly signposted. It has been dubbed the 'Venice of the North', and while this comparison is unfair to both places, it should be no surprise that canal cruises are one of the best ways of viewing the city: central Bruges has 10 km (6 miles) of canals, with 4 km (2½ miles) accessible by boat tour.

Bruges is the capital of West Flanders province, and Belgium's most popular tourist destination, so be prepared for large crowds in the summer. In describing the city's attractions, certain words spring to mind – 'charming', 'picturesque' and 'delightful', for instance. Bruges is all of these, which is why ambling through the city is such a pleasure. It is not built on a grand scale calculated to awe the visitor, but views crowd you on every side, and around each corner it seems there is something else to delight the eye and fire the imagination.

Paradoxically, it was Bruges' five centuries of economic decline that preserved the buildings we now enjoy – there was never any money to demolish and rebuild. The badly dilapidated city was 'discovered' by visitors in the 19th century, and in the quieter residential quarters you can still sense what it must have been like to walk through the forgotten streets of a forgotten town – your footsteps ringing on the cob-

Bruges' Bell Tower

> **Bruges' Old Town is almost an island encircled by canals. At the centre of the island and at the heart of the city's life is the Markt, Bruges' main square. All the city sights described in this chapter are within 2 km (1 mile) of the Markt**

The neo-Gothic spires of the 19th-century Provinciaal Hof

blestones while church bells chime and a horse's hooves echo from a nearby street.

One of the first things to strike visitors today is the harmonious appearance of the architecture. The characteristic step gables of the houses may be a bit worn through age, but this only adds to their charm. You'll notice that most buildings are of brick, with their shutters and woodwork painted in traditional Bruges red. Bruges is now so beautifully restored that you may briefly find yourself yearning for something less perfect just by way of contrast; Belgians themselves describe the place as an outdoor museum.

Still, you are all but certain to enjoy the walk described below; you should also take pleasure in improvising by discovering the city on your own (perhaps simply following the canals, or tracing the path of the city walls with their big, imposing gates). Horse-drawn carriages can also be hired.

Our walk begins at the **Markt**, Bruges' main square. Before you set off, take time to look around the Markt. This may be the 21st century (as the density of motor vehicles proves), but not much has changed since some of the civic buildings and houses that you can see were constructed; it's not hard to imagine what the place would have looked like in the city's bustling golden age.

SOUTH FROM THE MARKT

On the southeast side of the square, dominating the city, is the magnificent complex of brick buildings known as the **Belfort-Hallen** (Bell Tower and Covered Market; open Tues–Sun 9.30am–5pm; admission fee). One of the first priorities of any visitor is to ignore the 1-m (3-ft) lean of the 90-m (300-ft) belfry and climb its 366 steps for a breathtaking view of the town and surrounding countryside (the best time is early morning or late afternoon). The belfry dates from the 13th century, when Bruges was at the height of its prosperity, but the final storey (with the clock) is 15th-century. The second-floor houses a treasury where the town seal and charters were kept safely behind intricate Romanesque grilles (built in 1292), each requiring nine separate keys to open them.

You may already have heard the 47-bell carillon (which weighs 27 tons and hangs in the tower above). The belfry is an excellent landmark when you're finding your way around. The covered market and courtyard, also dating from the 13th century, would have been crammed with traders, the air heavy with the scent of spices brought by Venetian merchants. Originally, a canal lay below the covered market, which was used for the loading and unloading of goods. City statutes were announced from the balcony over the market entrance.

At the centre of the Markt is a 19th-century monument to the heroes of the Bruges Matins *(see page 12)*. **Pieter de Coninck and Jan Breydel are stained green with age, but they still look suitably determined.**

The 13th-century cloth halls were once located on the east side of the Markt, now the site of the neo-Gothic **Provinciaal Hof**, housing the West Flanders provincial government (not open to visitors). The **Craenenburg**, on the opposite side of the square, was where the Habsburg Crown Prince Maximilian of Austria was briefly imprisoned by the city in 1488; the future emperor, understandably disgruntled, did his best ever afterwards to promote trade through Antwerp at the expense of Bruges' economy *(see page 14)*. On the same side of the square, at the corner of Sint-Amandsstraat, is a beautiful 15th-century brick building, the **Huis Bouchoute**.

The Burg

A stroll down Breidelstraat, in the southeast corner of the Markt (next to the Halle), takes you past narrow De Garre, the shortest street in Bruges; if you need refreshment, there's a cosy 100-beer bar at the end, the Staminee de Garre. Breidelstraat leads to the **Burg**, one of Europe's finest medieval squares, named after the castle built by Baldwin Iron Arm.

Which building in the square is the most splendid? It's a hard choice. On the corner of Breidelstraat and the Burg is the ornate baroque **Proosdij** (Deanery), formerly the palace of the bishops of Bruges, dating from 1666. Its parapet is lined with urns and topped with a handsome female personification of justice armed with sword and scales. The building stands on the site of the demolished Sint-Donaaskerk (St Donatian's), a Carolingian-style church built around 950. A miniature stone replica of the church stood until recently (and may do so again) under the trees of the Burg.

The magnificent Stadhuis

The **Stadhuis** (Town Hall; open Tues–Sun 9.30am–5pm; admission fee) on the south side of the Burg was constructed between 1376

and 1420. It is one of the oldest town halls in Belgium and a Gothic masterpiece, its delicately traced windows framed within pilasters topped with octagonal turrets. If you stand close to the building, its statues and spiral chimneys seem to be curving down over you, the detailing of the sandstone façade becoming even more impressive. The statues on the façade (modern copies of those painted by Van Eyck and destroyed by the French in the 1790s) are of the counts of Flanders.

The superb vaulted oak ceiling of the Gothic Hall

The exterior of the Stadhuis promises great things, and the interior of the magnificent town hall will certainly not let you down. Bluestone stairs lead from the flag-draped entrance hall to the first-floor Gothic Hall, a splendid room that witnessed the first meeting of the States General, set up in 1464 by the dukes of Burgundy to regulate provincial contributions to the treasury. The vaulted oak ceiling (begun in 1385 and finished in 1402), with its preposterously long pendant keystones at the junctions of the arches, is richly decorated in tones of brown, black, maroon and gold, surrounding painted scenes from the New Testament.

The murals, depicting important events in the city's history, were painted by the De Vriendt brothers in 1905 after the original 1410 wall decorations were lost. The small, delicate balcony near the entrance door was for the town pipers and other musicians. The hall is used for civic ceremonies, receptions and weddings. An adjoining room displays old coins, documents and other artefacts relating to the history of Bruges.

To the right of the Stadhuis as you face it is the small gilded entrance to the **Heilig-Bloedbasiliek** (Basilica of the Holy Blood; open Apr–Sept 9.30am–noon and 2–6pm; Oct–Mar Thur–Tues 10am–noon and 2–4pm, Wed 10am–noon; admission fee). Its three-arched façade was completed by 1534, making it a mere youth in comparison with the Stadhuis. Its ornate stone carvings and gilded statues of angels, knights and their ladies stand below two closely adjoining and strangely Islamic-looking towers of great delicacy. The interior of the basilica is divided into two chapels, a 12th-century Romanesque lower chapel and a younger Gothic upper chapel, providing a dramatic contrast in styles. The lower chapel is a study in shadows, with austere, unadorned lines, typically uncompromising Romanesque pillars, and little decoration except for a relief carving over an interior doorway depicting the baptism of St Basil (an early Church Father). St Basil's relics were brought back from Palestine by Robert II, the Count of Flanders. The faded carving is child-like in style, its naivety emphasised by the two mismatched columns supporting it.

On Ascension Day every year, the holy relic is carried through Bruges in the famous Heilig-Bloed Processie (Procession of the Holy Blood), the most important of West Flanders' festivals. The venerated phial is transported in a flamboyant gold and silver reliquary that is normally kept in the treasury off the chapel.

Access to the upper chapel is through a beautiful

late-Gothic doorway. Ascending by an elegant, broad 16th-century spiral staircase, you can enter the upper chapel beneath the organ case. The lines of the chapel may have been spoiled somewhat by over-eager 19th-century decoration and murals, but the greater impression is of warmth and richness. The ceiling looks like an up-turned boat and the room is flooded with a golden light. The bronze-coloured pulpit is a curious sight, bearing a remarkable resemblance to a cored and stuffed tomato.

The Basilica of the Holy Blood: home to a venerated relic

In a small side chapel you'll find the holy relic from which the church derives its name. Flemish knight Dirk of Alsace returned from the Second Crusade in the Holy Land in 1149 and is said to have brought with him a crystal phial believed to contain some drops of Christ's blood. Soon venerated all over medieval Europe, it is still brought out each Friday for the faithful. The dried blood turned to liquid at regular intervals for many years, an event declared to be a miracle by Pope Clement V. The phial is stored in a richly and rather heavily ornate silver tabernacle presented by the archdukes of Spain in 1611.

Opposite the Basilica, the Bruges Tourist Office (indicated by a large white and green sign) occupies the **Landhuis van**

het Brugse Vrije (Liberty of Bruges Palace), an early 18th-century neoclassical building on the site of an older structure that formerly housed the law courts. (At the rear of the building overlooking the canal are the remains of an attractive 16th-century façade.)

The **Renaissancezaal Brugse Vrije** (Renaissance Hall of the Liberty of Bruges; open Tues–Sun 9.30am–5pm; admission fee), with its entrance at Burg 11a, has one main exhibit – the great black marble and oak Renaissance 'Emperor Charles' chimneypiece, designed by the painter Lanceloot Blondeel in tribute to Charles V, started in 1528 and finished in 1531. This is one of the most memorable artworks in Bruges: the carving is on a monumental scale, covering an entire wall and joining the ceiling with carved tendrils and caskets. A statue of Charles in full armour, wearing the emblem of the Order of the Golden Fleece, is in the centre. Forty-six coats of arms and ribbons of wood also appear on it. Among many of the scenes, the design depicts the defeat of the French at Pavia and the biblical story of Susanna and the Elders. The intricate craftsmanship of the piece is superb and quite overwhelming, but the handholds for gentlemen to use while drying their boots are the sort of domestic touch everyone remembers.

Fish for sale at the Vismarkt

Adjoining this building is the statue-laden, Renaissance-style **Oude Civiele Griffie** (Old Recorder's House), completed in 1537. Note how the sinuously curved and scrolled gables contrast with the older, linear step gables of most of the architecture found in Bruges.

Around Vismarkt

Wander through the Renaissance arch joining the Oude Civiele Griffie and the Stadhuis, and follow Blinde Ezelstraat across the bridge until you reach the colonnaded **Vismarkt** (fishmarket). Built in 1821, the market sells fresh fish from the North Sea along with varied craft items (open Tues–Sat 8am–1pm). Along both sides of the canal are pretty streets.

On Groene Rei (left at the bridge) you will find the 1634 **Pelikaanhuis** (Pelican House). Easily identified by its Pelican emblem over the doorway, this was once a hospital or alms-

The doorway to the Pelikaanhuis, formerly an almshouse

house. Such almshouses can be found all over Bruges: they were built by the guilds of the city to shelter the sick, elderly and poor. They are usually low, whitewashed cottages like the ones in Zwarte-Leertouwerstraat (take the last right turn in Groene Rei).

Back behind the Vismarkt, you can wander through Huidenvettersplein (Tanners' Square), which has become something of a growth area for cafés and excellent restaurants. **Huidevettershuis** (Tanners' Guild Hall), the turreted house (now a restaurant), was built in 1630.

Beyond the square, **Rozenhoedkaai** (Rosary Quay) is one of the places where boat tours depart; do stop to enjoy

See the best of the Flemish Primitives in the Groeninge Museum

the view from the quay. The River Dijver – a branch of the Reie – begins at **Sint-Jan Nepomucenusbrug** (St John of Nepomuk Bridge). A statue portrays the good man himself, appropriately the patron saint of bridges.

Along the bank, the tree-lined Dijver – site of a weekend flea market – passes superb old houses and crosses the canal into Gruuthusestraat. On the left is a complex of museums: the Groeninge, the Brangwyn and the Gruuthuse.

The Groeninge Museum

The **Groeninge Museum** (open Tues–Sun 9.30am–5pm; admission fee) contains some of the great works of the Flemish Primitives, including Van Eyck's portrait of his supercilious-looking wife Margareta, which is so typical of the painter's incredible realism, and Bosch's deeply disturbing *Last Judgement*, with the fires of hell ablaze. The *Judgement of Cambyses*, painted by Gerard David in

1498, depicts the judicial skinning of a corrupt judge while detached onlookers coolly observe the proceedings.

Other treasures include Memling's glorious *Moreel Tryptych* depicting St Christopher, with portraits in the side panels, and his *St John Altarpiece*. In addition, there are magnificent portraits by Hugo van der Goes, Rogier van der Weyden and Petrus Christus, as well as paintings by unknown masters, many of them depicting views of the city.

However, the greatest work in the museum is undoubtedly Van Eyck's *Madonna with Canon George van der Paele*, where the textures and folds of the clothing and carpets are reproduced with breathtaking effect.

There is also work from later periods, including a landscape by James Ensor, enigmatic work by René Magritte, and some more recently acquired Flemish Expressionists – but it's the early Flemish artists who steal the show.

The Brangwyn Museum

At number 16, the **Brangwyn Museum** (open Tues–Sun 9.30am–5pm; admission fee) is named after the extensive art collection of Sir Frank Brangwyn, a Welsh artist who was born in Bruges in 1867 and who

> Frank Brangwyn was a disciple of the Arts and Crafts Movement and apprentice to its greatest exponent, William Morris, before becoming a war artist in World War I.

bequeathed his work to the city when he died in 1956. The museum has a collection of paintings by Brangwyn and also some of his furniture, prints and rugs.

A small **Lace Museum** (open Tues–Sun 9.30am–5pm; admission fee) in the same building comprises a series of chandeliered apartments, each exhibiting incredibly detailed examples of the art of lace-making, particularly from the 19th century.

**Apocalyptic Horsemen in the
Brangwyn Museum courtyard**

The Gruuthuse Museum

In the courtyard at the rear of the Brangwyn Museum you can see Rik Poot's sculptures of the *Four Horsemen of the Apocalypse*, a scary combination of robotic armour and animal skeletons. The oldest bridge in Bruges (with a pronounced arch and cobblestones) connects the courtyard to the **Gruuthuse Museum** (open Tues–Sun 9.30am–5pm; admission fee), so called because the original owners had rights to tax the *gruut* used by brewers (the various herbs, spices and plants used in brewing beer before the introduction of hops).

The building itself is one of the museum's best exhibits – a splendid mansion of red brick. Built in the 15th century, it has twice sheltered fugitive English kings: both Henry IV and Charles II stayed here, in 1471 and 1656 respectively. Inside the house, beautifully furnished in a variety of period styles, there is an evocative smell of polished wood.

The museum has an exceptional collection of lacework, tapestries and musical instruments, including a delicate spinet. Items are labelled in Flemish only, but you do not need labels to admire the imposing medieval kitchen or the magnificent fireplace and beamed ceiling in Room 1. Room 5, with painted angels sculpted in the ceiling beams, provides some interesting views over the rooftops and into the courtyard of the mansion. There are also fine antique crossbows and a guillotine on display. Finally, the oratory (private chapel) leads to the chancel of the adjoining Church of Our Lady.

Church of Our Lady 35

Onze-Lieve-Vrouwekerk

The exterior of **Onze-Lieve-Vrouwekerk** (Church of Our Lady) is a hodge-podge of different styles and is slightly forbidding. More interesting is the interior, which is almost a warehouse of religious artworks and treasures (open Tues–Sat 9.30am–12.30pm and 1.30–5pm, Sun 1.30–5pm; admission fee to parts of the church). Chief among them is the *Madonna and Child* by Michelangelo, originally intended for Siena Cathedral and the only one of the sculptor's works to travel outside Italy during his lifetime. It was brought to Bruges by a Flemish merchant, Jan van Moeskroen. The Madonna is a subdued, preoccupied figure, while the infant leans nonchalantly on her knee.

Michelangelo's *Madonna and Child* in Onze-Lieve-Vrouwekerk

There are some fine paintings here by Pieter Pourbus (*Last Supper and Adoration of the Shepherds*) and Gerard David (*Transfiguration*), but it is the chancel area that holds most interest, after the Michelangelo. Here you can see the **tombs** of Charles the Bold and his daughter Mary of Burgundy, fine examples of, respectively, Renaissance and late-Gothic carving. Both sarcophagi are richly decorated with coats of arms linked with floral motifs in copper-gilt gold, reds and blues; the figures themselves (with domestic

The 122-m (400-ft) brick tower of Onze-Lieve-Vrouwekerk (the second highest in Belgium) once served as a kind of inland lighthouse for ships on their way to Bruges.

details like the pet dogs at Mary's feet) are also in copper gilt. Whether or not Charles and Mary are actually buried here is a matter of some dispute. Charles died in battle in Nancy in 1477 and it was difficult to identify the body. Mary (who died in a riding accident at the age of 25, bringing to a close the 100-year reign of the House of Burgundy) may in fact be buried among a group of polychromed tombs in the choir that were discovered in 1979. You can see the frescoed tombs beneath your feet through windows in the floor and by means of mirrors in front of the sarcophagi.

Elsewhere in the church, you'll find the funerary chapel of Pieter Lanchals *(see page 40)*, containing frescoed tombs in maroon and black, as well as Van Dyck's starkly atmospheric painting of Christ on the Cross. The splendid wooden gallery connecting the church to the adjacent Gruuthuse Museum *(see page 34)* dates from the 15th century.

Sint-Janshospitaal

Opposite the church and through an archway you will find **Sint-Janshospitaal** (St John's Hospital). Constructed in the 12th century, this is the oldest building in Bruges, and, in what were once the wards of the hospital, there is an exhibition of historical documents and rather alarming surgical instruments. The 17th-century pharmacy has a carved relief showing patients sleeping two to a bed. Amazingly, the hospital was still functioning in the 19th century, and there is a strong sense of tradition in the place, enhanced by the informative visitor centre (which also has an internet café).

The Memlingmuseum

Housed in the old hospital church the **Memlingmuseum** ◄
(open Tues–Sun 9.30am–5pm; admission fee), is largely
devoted to six masterpieces by the Flemish master Hans
Memling. The museum is very small but is highly recommended. Each of the exhibited works displays Memling's
captivating attention to detail and mastery of realism. It's
impossible to pick the 'best', but probably the most famous
is the detailed *Reliquary of St Ursula*, one of the greatest art
treasures in the country. Commissioned by two sisters who
worked in the church, the reliquary is in the form of a miniature Gothic chapel with Memling's painted panels in the positions of the windows.

The *Mystic Marriage of St Catherine* includes St John the
Evangelist and St John the Baptist, both patron saints of the
hospital: it has been suggested that saints Catherine and Bar-

The canal frontage of Sint-Janshospitaal, Bruges' oldest building

Memling's *Reliquary of St Ursula*, a national treasure

bara are portraits of Mary of Burgundy and Margaret of York. A painting by Jan Beerbloch depicts the relaxed standards of hospital hygiene of the time: nurses sweep the floors while dogs wander the dormitories.

Around Mariastraat

If you head south along Mariastraat and look left along Nieuwe Gentweg, you will see some typical white almshouses, which have gardens open to the public. The next turning on the right is Walstraat, a peaceful street of delightful 16th- and 17th-century gabled houses where lacemaking is still practised (outside on warm days).

If your thirst for culture is overtaken by a thirst for something else, a short stroll will bring you to **De Halve Maan Brewery** (open Apr–Sept daily, guided tours hourly 10am–5pm; Oct–Mar daily, guided tours 11am and 3pm; fee for guided tours) at Walplein 26. Belgium is well known for its many hundreds of beers, and Bruges beers are exceptionally good. De Halve Maan ('The Half Moon') has been brewing in the city since 1564 and today produces a light, highly fermented local beer called Straffe Hendrik (Flemish for 'Strong Henry', after its high alcohol content). The 45-minute guided tour of the brewery museum will reveal how it's all done, and also includes an ascent to the roof, affording a good view over the gables of central Bruges. The building is suffused with a sweet smell from the brewing process. At the end of the visit, each visitor receives a drink in the congenial bar, lined with every conceivable shape of beer bottle.

The Begijnhof

South of the church along Mariastraat, follow the signposts to the **Begijnhof**. Belgium is famous for the number of its residences for tertiary religious orders, which were for unmarried or abandoned women (known as Beguines) who wished to live under religious rule without having to commit themselves to the full vows of a nun. The women cared for the sick and made a living by lacemaking.

The **Prinselijk Begijnhof ten Wijngaarde** (Princely Beguinage of the Vineyard) was founded in 1245 by Margaret of Constantinople and remained a Beguine residence until very recently – it is now a Benedictine convent. The nuns wear the traditional clothes of the Beguines and maintain some of their predecessors' customs. The convent is one of the most attractive Beguine residences. Reached by a bridge over the canal and through an arch, it comprises a circle of white, 17th-century houses set around a courtyard of grass and trees that comes alive with daffodils each spring. In a city replete with picturesque views, this is one of the most photographed places in Bruges. You can enter one of the former houses, which is now a small museum, and the church, built originally in 1245.

Around the Begijnhof the layout of the streets is as it was in the 17th century, so take time to wander around and enjoy the views. This is also the spot where the hard-working carriage horses of Bruges stop to enjoy a well-earned rest mid-tour, together with a drink of water pumped from a horse's head statue.

The Half Moon brewery sign

The presence of swans on Minnewater, so the story goes, stems from the time in 1448 when Emperor Maximilian was imprisoned in Bruges and his councillor Pieter Lanchals was beheaded. Lanchals' coat of arms featured a swan, and the emperor ordered that swans be kept on the canals of Bruges for ever more, as a reminder of the city's dreadful crime.

Minnewater

The picturesque and under-standably popular park and lake of **Minnewater** (Lake of Love) lie to the south of Walplein and Wijngaard-plein. The lake was originally the inner harbour of Bruges, before the Zwin inlet silted up and cut off the city from the sea; you can still see the 15th-century Sashuis (lock house). Beyond the Sashuis, the tower on the right is the Poertoren (Powder Tower), a remnant of old fortifications.

The 'Lake of Love' – picturesque Minnewater

Katelijnestraat

Just east of Minnewater, at Katelijnestraat 43, is the **Diamantmuseum Brugge** (Bruges Diamond Museum: daily 10.30am–5.30pm; admission fee). The museum documents the history of diamond polishing – a technique thought to have been invented by the Bruges goldsmith, Lodewijk van Berquem, in the mid-15th century. On display you'll

Sint-Salvatorskathedraal is Bruges' oldest parish church

find a reconstruction of van Berquem's workshop, examples of tools and machinery used in diamond polishing, plus models, paintings and rare rock samples. Daily demonstrations (at 12.15pm) further illustrate the technique.

Steenstraat and 't Zand Square

Return to the Markt via Mariastraat, Simon Stevinplein and Steenstraat, a beautiful street lined with gabled guild-houses. The Boat House and Mason's House on this street are topped with a gilded boat and bear, and masonic instruments, respectively. If you turn left on Steenstraat, you will come to **Sint-Salvatorskathedraal** (Holy Saviour's Cathedral; open Mon–Sat 10–11.30am and 2–5pm, Sun 3–5pm; closed to casual visitors during services; admission fee. Museum open Sun 3–5pm, Mon–Fri 2–5pm; admission fee).

The oldest parish church in Bruges, it has been a cathedral since 1834, replacing the city-centre cathedral destroyed by the French in the late 18th century. Parts of the building date from the 12th and 13th centuries, though the church was originally founded in the 10th century.

> **'t Zand Square was chosen as the site of the city's new concert hall, the Concertgebouw Brugge, the main focus of Bruges' year as European City of Culture in 2002.**

The Gothic interior of the church is quite spartan and curiously unfocused in design, but the choir stalls and the baroque rood screen showing God the Father are worth a look. The cathedral has its own museum, located off the right transept. Specialising in liturgical objects, it is worth visiting for its Flemish paintings, including work by Dirk Bouts and Pieter Pourbus.

Continuing along Zuidzandstraat, you come to bustling 't Zand, a square with many hotels and cafés. The square is also notable for its fountain and groups of modern sculpture by Stefaan Depuydt and Livia Canestraro. The four female figures in *Bathing Women* symbolise Antwerp, Bruges, Kortrijk and Ghent; *Landscape of Flanders* is an abstract representation of the region's flat landscape; *The Cyclists* is an expression of youth and hope for the future; and *The Fishermen* represents Bruges' ancient ties with the sea.

Returning to Steenstraat will lead you back to the Markt. If you make a short detour south of Simon Stevinplein to Oude Burg, you will find the **Hof van Watervliet**. The 16th-century buildings have been much restored, but are still of interest, with former residents including the humanist scholar Erasmus and the exiled Charles II of England.

NORTH FROM THE MARKT

The city north of the Markt used to be home to the merchants of medieval Bruges. It was also where they conducted their business, for it was common practice to live and work in the same building. The avenues of elegant houses from this period are punctuated with grandiose mansions dating from the 18th century, and the canals here meet and diverge in broad highways of water – it is no wonder many visitors regard this part as their favourite section of the city.

Jan van Eyckplein

Just a few minutes' walk north from the Markt along Vlamingstraat will lead you to Jan van Eyckplein and adjoining Spiegelrei. Bruges has many former harbours, and this one was the busiest of them all; the canal that terminates here once led to the Markt. It was also the commercial and diplomatic centre for medieval Bruges, and foreign consulates opened along the length of Spiegelrei.

There is a statue of the painter in the square, but it is the buildings that really stand out. Jan looks directly at the most striking of these, called the **Poorters Loge** (Burghers' Lodge). The pencil tower may point heavenwards, but the building was in fact the meeting place of the wealthier merchants of Bruges. It dates from the 14th century; on its façade there is a statue of the jolly bear that features in the city's coat of arms. It was also the emblem of a jousting club that held its events in the marketplace outside.

To the right of the Poorters Loge is the 15th-century **Oud Tolhuis** (Old Customs House), where tolls were

Jan van Eyck looks down on the square that bears his name

levied by the dukes of Luxembourg, whose coats of arms are on the façade. This fine Gothic building now holds the city archives, comprising 100,000 volumes and 600 manuscripts.

East of Jan van Eyckplein

From Jan van Eyckplein you can wander through the lovely street of Spinolarei into Koningstraat and Sint-Maartensplein, where you'll find **Sint-Walburgakerk** (Church of St Walburga). This is an impressive baroque church, built in 1643 by the Bruges Jesuit Pieter Huyssens, with a statue of St Francis Xavier standing above the entrance door. The baroque interior is for the most part quite unremarkable, except for the fabulous pulpit by Artus Quellin the Younger, which has twin stairways leading to a pulpit with a scalloped canopy uplifted by trumpeting angels.

By crossing the canal and following Sint-Annarei south into Sint-Annakerkstraat, you will see the slender spire of **Sint-Annakerk** (Church of St Anne), a 1624 baroque replacement for the Gothic church demolished in 1561. Inside, the baroque carving of the rood screen, confessionals and pulpit, as well as the rich panelling, are all well worth viewing if you have time (and if the church is open).

Skulls and bones adorn the altar of the Jeruzalemkerk

The unusual tower with the vaguely Oriental look visible from Sint-Annakerk belongs to the **Jeruzalemkerk**, located in Peperstraat. The church is named after and modelled on the Church of the Holy Sepulchre in Jerusalem. Dating from 1428, it was built by the Adornes family, originally merchants from Genoa, who had travelled on a pilgrimage to Jerusalem and were so impressed by the church that they built this one in Bruges. There is even a copy of Christ's memorial tomb in the crypt.

It is a sombre, stark and constricted church with very good examples of 15th- and 16th-century stained glass, some of which depicts members of the Adornes family. In the nave you can see effigies of Anselmus Adornes and his wife. The altar is carved in a rather macabre fashion, with skulls and bones, and the cave-like atmosphere of the church is emphasised by the space behind the altar and above the crypt, which rises almost to the full height of the tower to create a rather eerie, artificial-looking cavern.

Beside the Jeruzalemkerk is the **Kantcentrum** (Lace Centre; open Mon–Fri 10am–noon and 2–6pm, Sat 10am–noon

Ancient Handicraft

Lace-making by hand in Bruges, an industry which at its peak in the 1840s provided steady employment – and low wages – for 10,000 local women and girls, is making a slow but steady comeback, thanks mainly to the demand from visiting tourists. Even in its heyday, lace-making was a cottage industry. Handmade lace is expensive, and most of the lace sold in the city's multitude of lace shops today is machine-made and imported.

The most popular kind of lace made in Bruges is bobbin lace, created using a technique developed in Flanders in the 16th century. Threads of silk, linen or cotton on as many as 700 different bobbins are crossed and braided around a framework of pins. It takes great skill and concentration to do this and it's fascinating to watch an experienced craftswoman (it generally is a woman) at work. Other styles of handmade Belgian lace are *bloemenwerk* (flower lace), *rozenkant* (pearled rosary) and *toveressesteek* (fairy stitch).

Lace is still made the traditional way at the Kantcentrum

and 2–5pm; admission fee). This museum and workshop is situated in the 15th-century Jeruzalem-godshuizen (almshouses) founded by the Adornes family. Here, fine examples of the craft of lace-making and demonstrations by the workers and their students can be seen every day.

A sign points down Balstraat towards the **Stedelijk Museum voor Volkskunde** (Folklore Museum; open Tues–Sun 9.30am–5pm; admission fee). The museum, at Rolweg 40, is housed in a delightful row of 17th-century whitewashed almshouses built by the cobblers' guild, and the life of everyday West Flanders is recreated in the traditionally furnished interiors, including a primary school class, cooper's and milliner's workshops, a sweet shop and everyday household scenes. A traditional ale house – De Zwarte Kat (The Black Cat) – offers some respite for the weary walker.

West of Jan van Eyckplein

If you return to Jan van Eyckplein, you can then follow Acadamiestraat from the west side of the square. It joins Grauwerkerstraat, where you will find the elegant **Huis ter Beurze**. Now a bank, the 15th-century house belonged to the Van der Beurze family. They leased rooms to many merchants of the city, who lived and worked in the house; the family's name (rendered as 'bourse' or 'beurs') has since come to designate the place for a commercial stock exchange in many languages. The Genoese merchants in Bruges did their business in the building opposite, the

Natiehuis van Genua (Nation House of Genoa), built in 1441 and now housing a chic restaurant.

North of the Markt, there are no grand churches to compare with Onze-Lieve-Vrouwekerk or Sint-Salvatorskathedraal, but **Sint-Jakobskerk** (St James's Church; open Apr–Sept daily 9.30am–5pm; Oct–Mar Tues–Sun 9.30am–5pm; closed to casual visitors during services; admission fee) in Sint-Jakobsstraat probably makes the most determined bid for grandiosity. Thanks to generous gifts from the dukes of Burgundy, the 13th-century Gothic church was improved and enlarged to its present size. It has a pleasing internal harmony strangely lacking in many of the other churches in Bruges, and is illuminated by a pale pink light when the sun is shining. The interior is decorated with an abundance of 16th–18th-century paintings and tombs.

Sint-Jakobskerk looks down on Sint-Jakobsstraat

The glorious canopied pulpit is worth a closer inspection for its intricate, skilful carving. Among the most interesting of the tombs is the two-tiered arrangement of Ferry de Gros and his two wives. De Gros, who died in 1544, was a treasurer of the Order of the Golden Fleece. The tomb is reminiscent of the Italian Renaissance, with ornate floral designs on the ceramic wall-tiles. Outside, Sint-Jakobsstraat leads directly back to the Markt.

TRIPS FROM BRUGES

After the near perfection of Bruges, any other town in the region can seem disappointing, but there are several places of interest that you may like to explore on your way to or from the city. Most of them are no more than a few miles from Bruges. The exceptions are the World War I battlefields around Ypres (Ieper) – there are organised coach trips, but you may prefer to drive yourself – and Veurne. For descriptions of Brussels, Antwerp and Belgium's coastal resorts, see the *Berlitz Pocket Guide to Brussels* and the *Berlitz Pocket Guide to Belgium*.

Damme

The attractive approach-roads to this picturesque village, located 7 km (4 miles) northeast of Bruges, are lined with pollarded trees, all kinked in exactly the same spot by the prevailing wind that blows across the open countryside. Once the outer port of its larger neighbour, **Damme** still retains an air of medieval prosperity, with some fine old buildings and excellent restaurants around its marketplace. With a windmill and skating on the canal in winter, Damme is the epitome of a typical Flemish village.

Damme's one main street (Kerkstraat) has a delightful **Stadhuis** (town hall) with four corner turrets, built in 1468.

> In the summer, you can take a paddle-boat canal cruise from Noorwegse Kaai in Bruge to Damme. Alternatively, take a No 4 bus from the railway station – or walk or cycle along the canalside paths.

In front of the building stands a statue of the poet Jacob van Maerlant (1230–96), who wrote his most important works in Damme. The white sandstone façade is adorned with further statues of various historic notables including Duke Charles the Bold and Margaret of

York. At one corner, two 'stones of justice' hang from the wall. They used to be tied to the neck or feet of unfortunate women who had given offence in some way, and who were then made to parade round the village.

To the right of the building as you face it is **De Grote Sterre** (The Great Star), a twin-gabled 15th-century house that became the home of the Spanish governor in the 17th century. Almost destroyed in a storm in 1990, it has undergone extensive restoration. It now houses the Tourist Information Office. Four doors further down, at number 13, is the 15th-century house where the wedding party of Charles the Bold and Margaret of York was held in 1468. Royal weddings were celebrated in lavish style: in Bruges the festivities lasted two weeks.

Sint-Janshospitaal (St John's Hospital) is across the road and down from the Stadhuis. Founded in 1249, it includes a

Even modest villages such as Damme often have a splendid *Stadhuis*

You can take a paddle-boat from Bruges to Damme

baroque chapel and a museum of paintings, liturgical objects and sacred books.

Further up the street and visible from the museum is the 13th-century tower of one of Bruges' prominent beacons, the **Onze-Lieve-Vrouwekerk** (Church of Our Lady). The church has endured many vicissitudes down the centuries, including a fire started in 1578 by soldiers of the Prince of Orange. The tower, gaining its present appearance as a result of partial demolition in 1725, is now the haunt of stray weeds and jackdaws. The separate nave, which has been restored, can be visited in the summer months, when the site seems rather less menacing.

Signposts will lead you to the town's former herring market, which comprises an attractive circle of whitewashed cottages surrounding the village's first drinking-water pump.

Veurne

A small town (with a population not much greater than that of Damme), just 6 km (4 miles) from the border with France, Veurne grew from a 9th-century fortress and now has an attractive central marketplace, among the best in Belgium. The town's *Boetprocessie* (Procession of the Penitents) takes place on the last Sunday in July, presenting scenes from Christ's Passion. Owing much to Spanish influence (the town once served as a Spanish garrison), the procession is similar to the Spanish celebration of *Semana Santa* (Holy Week). There are also other processions during Easter and Lent.

Most of Veurne's places of interest are in or alongside the central Grote Markt, where you'll also find plenty of cafés and restaurants. Tickets for guided tours and carriage rides through the town are available in the summer months from the tourist office in the square.

The typical yellow Flemish brick is much in evidence, together with an architectural style that shows the Spanish presence in its restraint. The gabled **Stadhuis** (town hall) in the Grote Markt, built in 1612, has an attractive loggia of bluestone contrasting with the yellow brick of the rest of the structure. The building is open to visitors; among its fine interiors are some unusual and impressive leather wall hangings originating from Córdoba in southern Spain.

The **Landhuis**, adjoining the Stadhuis, was built in 1616, its Gothic bell-tower topped with a baroque spire. Next door is a delightful parade of five houses with step gables, each with a different design of columns around the windows. The cafés on the ground floors spill out into the square on warm days. On the northeast side of the square is the **Spanish Pavilion** which, as the name suggests, was the headquarters for Spanish officers during the 17th century. Across the road, the building with all the window shutters is the Renaissance **Vleeshuis** (Meat Market), built in 1615, and now a library.

Veurne stands on the junction of several canals

The imposing, unfinished tower of **Sint-Niklaaskerk** (Church of St Nicholas), rising from nearby Appelmarkt, can be climbed for the view; the 13th-century structure has a carillon. The

Elegant Tillegem Castle

other church in the town is **Sint-Walburgakerk**, construction of which began in 1250 with ambitious plans that eventually proved too much for the little town. It has a splendid 27-m (90-ft) nave. The interior of the church is worth a visit, more for its overall effect than for any specific item, though there is a fine baroque pulpit.

Tillegembos

Bus number 25 will take you to the woods of Tillegembos in Bruges' southwestern suburb, Sint-Michiels. They cover an area of 80 hectares (200 acres), providing a real rural retreat if you need a break from the city. Lots of well-marked footpaths take you around this former estate, and there is a lakeside inn and play areas for children. An elegant, moated **castle** dating from the 14th century is today the headquarters of the West Flanders Tourist Office.

Kasteel Loppem

Situated just 3 km (2 miles) south of Bruges, the **Kasteel** (castle) at Loppem is a fine example of neo-Gothic architecture, conceived by August Pugin (architect of the British Houses of Parliament) and later completed by Jean Béthune. Built between 1858 and 1863, the structure appears from a distance to be a mass of verticals, all eaves and roof and pinnacles, accentuated by its reflection in the lake before it. Inside, the house is sumptuously decorated, the tone dominated by the wood of the ceilings and furniture. It has a private chapel and a wonderful, soaring hall.

Ypres and Flanders Fields

Southwest of Bruges towards the border with France lies **Flanders Fields**, a vast area of countryside that witnessed military carnage on an unprecedented scale. Although the senseless waste of millions of lives in World War I has gone down in history, the staggering numbers killed nevertheless still have the power to shock. Row upon row of gravestones in the many cemeteries of the area testify to the butchery of war. Whether or not you have relatives buried here, the peacefulness of the place and the solidarity in death of troops from all sides make for a moving and strangely comforting experience – the soldiers' ordeal is at an end.

Ypres (Ieper) is a name that still resonates in the collective memory. The focus of repeated attacks and counter-attacks, it was shelled to destruction during World War I, then carefully reconstructed over the next 40 years. Nothing old remains in the bustling town, but it has an open, relaxed central Grote Markt and an imposing Stadhuis. The **In Flanders Fields Museum** (open Apr–Sept daily 10am–6pm; Oct–Jan 8 and Feb–Mar Tues–Sun 10am–5pm; admission fee) in the Stadhuis is worth a visit if you have the time – the limitations of the exhibition are overcome by some powerful images of

---

Tours of Remembrance

There are coach tours available from Bruges that visit selected towns, war cemeteries and memorials. Alternatively, if you wish to take more time and follow your own inclinations, it is worth taking a car (or even a bicycle) and making use of 'Route 14–18', a carefully signposted route through the battlefield area of the Ypres Salient. It should be stressed, however, that nothing much remains of the battlefields. Where you wish to go will depend on your interests and on any family connections you may have with the war, and our survey of sites is necessarily selective.

images of the devastated countryside, and by pitiful mementos such as banknotes, caps, badges and buttons.

The **Menin Gate** memorial, located just off the Grote Markt, is built on a cutting through which thousands of men made their way towards the Ypres Salient. Designed by Reginald Blomfield, it comprises a classical façade fronting a vast arch with three open ceiling portals. It is inscribed with the names of nearly 55,000 British soldiers who died in battle but have no known graves.

Just southeast of Ypres, near Zillebeeke, on **Hill 62** stands a memorial to the Canadian troops who lost their lives. Near the hill, **Sanctuary Wood Cemetery** preserves a few remaining parts of trenches. At **Hill 60** a little further beyond Zillebeke, a roadside memorial commemorates the fallen of Australia, behind which lies a field of mounds and hollows, created by intensive bombardment, where you can still make out the ruins of bunkers. This 'strategically important' hill was constantly taken and retaken throughout World War I. Today, sheep graze here and birds sing in the trees.

A little over 10 km (6 miles) northeast of Ypres, situated off the N332 before Passendale (Passchendaele), is **Tyne Cot Military Cemetery**. Designed by the architect Sir Herbert Baker, the cemetery was intended to evoke the appearance of a traditional English graveyard, with white gravestones standing honourably in regular formation on a neat green lawn. Its large Cross of Sacrifice in Portland stone is built on the site of the Tyne Cot dressing station that was finally captured by Australian troops in 1917. The

Tyne Cot Cemetery has nearly 12,000 gravestones, the unidentified graves simply inscribed: 'A soldier of the Great War, known unto God'. The semi-circular wall at the top of the cemetery bears the names of 35,000 soldiers whose remains were never found.

Tyne Cot is the largest military cemetery in the world

slight rise on which the cemetery is located affords a view over the now peaceful countryside.

The German cemetery located at **Langemark**, approximately 16 km (10 miles) north of Ypres, contains the remains of more than 44,000 German soldiers – over half of them in a mass grave. It is referred to as the Students' Cemetery because so many young soldiers perished in the Ypres Salient in 1914 and 1915. The gravestones are simple tablets that lie flush with the lawn, on ground sheltered by mature trees. The cemetery contains the remnants of three bunkers.

Further northwest, 4 km (2½ miles) outside the town of Diksmuide, **Vladslo** German cemetery is the site of over 25,000 German graves and an extremely moving memorial sculpture by Käthe Kollwitz entitled *Grieving Parents*. The sculptor's son lies buried there. In fact, there are more than 150 war cemeteries in the area, making it seem as if Flanders Fields belong more to the dead than to the living.

WHERE TO GO IN GHENT

Ghent, the capital of East Flanders, lies at the confluence of the rivers Scheldt and Leie. The city is a little larger than Bruges, but most of its historic attractions are clustered together within walking distance of one another. But in contrast to its near neighbour and traditional economic rival, it is a city with more on its mind than just the tourist industry. Though it suffered the same economic decline as Bruges, historically it has been more successful in cultivating new sources of income and wealth, particularly in the 19th century, when the industrialisation of the country worked to Ghent's advantage.

Today, it is a city built on diverse economic interests, with the sense to preserve its historical heart – a city confident in its future and proud of its past. That past is shown in some magnificent buildings, second only to Bruges in their splendour. Many of them are being renovated and there is still much to do, but the various states of decay and refurbishment of the old buildings add to the excitement of discovery and a sense that Ghent is on the move. The inland port city has an almost Mediterranean air about it, with cafés and bars spilling out onto the sidewalks at the hint of warm weather.

Our tour starts from Sint-Baafsplein. Most of Ghent's historic Inner Town lies northwest of this square, straddling the Y-shaped meeting of the two rivers. This area is one of winding streets and alleyways, while the south is lined with elegant boulevards and imposing mansions.

Houses along Ghent's Korenlei

> **Like Bruges, Ghent offers canal boat cruises in summer. It is also fun to tour the city by tram: the main tram terminus is outside Sint-Pieters train station.**

SINT-BAAFSPLEIN

Standing in Sint-Baafsplein you can see Sint-Baafs-kathedraal on its east side, the Belfry and Lakenhalle on the west side, and the Royal Flemish Theatre on the north. To the south stands a memorial to Jan Frans Willems (1793–1846), who founded the Flemish movement. The oldest theatre in Ghent stood on the site of the **Hof Hamelinck** at number 10, constructed in 1739 (it's the house with the bust of the goddess Juno in its gable).

Sint-Baafskathedraal

The largely Gothic brick and granite **Sint-Baafskathedraal** was built over several centuries, the chancel dating from the turn of the 14th century, both the tower and the nave from the 15th century, and the transept from the mid-16th century. This magnificent structure is the first among many churches well worth visiting in Ghent, for the building itself, as well as for the treasures it contains.

The airy nave of the cathedral is an invigorating sight for even the most foot-sore visitor. A forest of stone bathed in light leads the eye onward and upward to a glorious Late-Gothic display of rib vaulting in the roof high above. The tower, providing some splendid views, also contains a carillon, while the crypt retains some of the original structure of an earlier Romanesque church.

Sint-Baafskathedraal is open daily Apr–Oct 8.30am–6pm; Nov–Mar 8.30am–5pm; admission is free. The Mystic Lamb Chapel is open Apr–Oct Mon–Sat 9.30am–4.45pm, Sun 1–4.30pm; Nov–Mar Mon–Sat 10.30am–3.45pm, Sun 1–3.30pm.

The cathedral's (and also the city's – and probably even the nation's) greatest treasure, is located in a side chapel to the left of the main entrance. Variously known as the *Ghent Altarpiece* or *The Adoration of the Mystic Lamb*, this marvellous panel painting is regarded as the crowning achievement of Jan van Eyck's Gothic style.

To art historian E.H. Gombrich, Van Eyck in this painting completed 'the final conquest of reality' in the northern Gothic tradition. Van Eyck did not investigate the principles of perspective scientifically like contemporary Italian masters – for example, the keyboard that the angel plays in the inside right-hand panel has almost no depth to it at all. What he did

The Ghent Altarpiece – humanity, optimism and remarkable realism

achieve, rather, was the accumulation of so much closely observed detail that he broke completely with medieval ideas and styles and instituted a new kind of realism.

The altarpiece seems to become increasingly detailed the closer you look at it. Look closely at the horses and people: they are real creatures of flesh and blood. His flowers and trees are astonishingly accurate; his portraits of the donors on the outside panels look like mercilessly truthful records of living individuals with all their imperfections. The painting as a whole is invested with a wonderful humanity and optimism, with God the Father, wise and beneficent, looking kindly upon all. If you look carefully, you will also

Who painted the Altarpiece?

Whether or not Jan van Eyck really was responsible for *The Adoration of the Mystic Lamb* has in the past been a matter of some dispute. An inscription on the frame of the altarpiece declares that it was started by a Hubert van Eyck and completed by his brother Jan. However, since no one has any other evidence for the existence of Hubert, it is thought by many that he was the mythical creation of Ghent citizens jealous of Bruges' monopolising of Jan. Certainly, it is difficult to believe that an artist of Van Eyck's genius could be surpassed by someone who has otherwise left nothing to posterity, and most art historians today unhesitatingly attribute the work of this painting solely to the master artist Jan van Eyck.

see Bruges Cathedral in the background of the central panel.

There are many other important works of art to be seen in the cathedral. Rubens' painting of 1624, *The Conversion of St Bavo* in the far left-hand side of the chancel, is full of the unique drama with which the artist infused all his work; it also contains a self-portrait in the red-cloaked convert. Just beyond the transept on the right-hand side of the chancel is Frans Pourbus the Elder's *Christ Among the Doctors*, painted in 1571. A youthful Jesus is shown amazing the elders of the temple with his knowledge and wisdom, but it is his audience that claims our attention: Pourbus portrayed contemporary luminaries such as Philip II and Charles V, Thomas Calvin, and even his rival, painter Pieter Breughel the Elder in the crowd. Down in the crypt is the striking *Calvary Tryptych* of Justus van Gent, painted in 1466 and clearly owing a debt of gratitude to Van Eyck in its precise attention to detail.

You will also find splendid examples of sculpture, the best of which is the baroque oak and marble pulpit, one of Laurent Delvaux's masterpieces, completed in 1741. The dynamic, intricate carving of the design sweeps the eye up to where the preacher would stand, above which a marble tree of knowledge grows complete with gilded serpent and fruit. St Bavo himself is commemorated in the baroque high altar of sculptor Hendrik Frans Verbruggen.

The Belfort and Lakenhalle

Opposite the cathedral, the **Belfort** (Belfry), completed in 1380, has since become the pre-eminent symbol of the city's independence (open mid-Mar–mid-Nov daily 10am–1pm and 2–6pm; admission fee). From March until November, a vertiginous lift ascent to the top of the 91-m (298-ft) tower will reward you with spectacular views across the city.

The towering Belfry

The gilded copper dragon at the top of the spire was first installed upon completion of the tower, but the creature and the four figures now poised at the corners of the viewing platform are modern replicas. The spire itself was restored at the beginning of the 20th century according to the original 14th-century design. The impressive workings of the clock and the 52-bell carillon can be closely inspected on the fourth floor of the tower.

On the north side of the Belfort stands the former prison, which has above its doorway the *Mammelokker*,

> **Ghent's Tourist
> Information Office is
> based in the crypt of
> the Belfort. It is open
> daily Apr–Oct 9.30am–
> 6.30pm; Nov–Mar
> 9.30am–4pm.**

a carved relief symbolic of Christian charity. This shows the old man Cimon, who has been condemned to death by starvation, being suckled by his daughter.

Together with the Belfort, the neighbouring **Laken-halle** (Cloth Hall) magnificently expresses Ghent's civic pride and wealth. The building, much restored, dates from 1441, once serving as the meeting place for the city's wool and cloth traders. Sadly, the interior is today relatively empty, though there is a short audio-visual display devoted to Ghent's history.

NORTH OF SINT-BAAFSPLEIN

Botermarkt and Hoogpoort

Across the road from the Lakenhalle in Botermarkt stands the rather formidable **Stadhuis** (Town Hall) – all pilasters and windows. It was built over a long period and in different styles, but manages to retain a surprising degree of architectural unity. The Stadhuis is like a giant calendar of architecture: the oldest part of the building (on the Hoog-poort side) dates from the early 16th century and, with its florid design and ornate statues, follows the style of Bruges' Stadhuis. Religious disputes in 1539, associated with the end of the wool trade and the economic decline of Ghent, halted the work for some 60 years, so Rombout Kelder-mans' design (incorporating statues in every conceivable niche and an ornate way with windows) was never complet-ed. Work began again with the Renaissance-style façade of the Botermarkt side of the hall; it was continued in the 18th century with the baroque façade facing the corner of Hoogpoort and Stadhuissteeg and the rococo Poeljemarkt side. The throne room and an impressive city council room are accessible inside. Guided tours (May–Oct Mon–Thu 3pm; admission fee) are well worth joining.

North from St Baafsplein, Hoogpoort runs northwest past some beautiful Ghent houses. On the corner with the square stands **Sint-Jorishof**, the former house of the Guild of Crossbowmen (now a hotel), built in 1477. It was in this house that Mary of Burgundy granted a charter of freedoms to the Flemish cloth towns *(see page 14)*.

At Hoogpoort 10 is **De Ram**. This house, built in 1732, was formerly home to an apothecary. A lamp (the traditional emblem of apothecaries) is carved in the façade, as are relief portraits of the botanist Carolus Clusius (who introduced the tulip to the Low Countries). A few doors down from De Ram, music emanates from Ghent's Royal Conservatory of

You can visit the Council Room in a guided tour of the Stadhuis

Music – during term time, you will see students carrying a variety of musical instruments around the streets.

Around Groentenmarkt and Korenmarkt

Hoogpoort will lead you to Groentenmarkt, site of the medieval pillory and former fishmarket. The **Groot Vleeshuis**, on the west side of the square, comprises a complex of gabled buildings restored in 1912 but dating from 1406. The buildings include a covered meat market, a guild-house and a chapel.

Korenmarkt (Corn Market) connects via Kortemunt with Groentenmarkt; at its southern end stands the landmark **Sint-Niklaaskerk** (St Nicholas' Church), from where Sint-Michielsbrug (St Michael's Bridge) spans the Leie River. The oldest parts of the Gothic Sint-Niklaaskerk date back to the 13th century, but the building was not completed until

Cross the Leie River on Sint-Michielsbrug to Sint-Michielskerk

the 18th century. Inside, the baroque high altar is a typically energetic design of the period. The whole church is flooded with a beautiful light on sunny days. Various guilds and 'De Fonteyne' (a kind of debating society for those who fancied themselves as orators) shared a chapel here; their meeting house is situated behind the church at Goudenleeuwplein 7, built in 1539 in Renaissance style.

This area offers some of the most characteristic views of Ghent; you can make out the towers of the Belfry and Sint-Baaf's, the picturesque Korenlei and Graslei quaysides, and the ominous mass of Gravensteen castle. Across from the bridge you will see **Sint-Michielskerk** (St Michael's Church), which acts as a kind of visual counterbalance to Sint-

> **Sint-Michielskerk contains a melancholy** *Crucifixion* **(1629) by Antoon van Dyck, more famous for his portraits than his religious works.**

Niklaaskerk. Adjacent to the church in Onderbergen there is a former Dominican monastery, known as **Het Pand**. The oldest parts of this harmonious complex of buildings – now owned and used by Ghent's university – date back to the 13th century. The monks could not have picked a more agreeable place to live.

Korenlei and Graslei

North from Sint-Michielsbrug, you can stroll on both banks of the river, past a splendid array of medieval guild-houses on the quaysides. **Korenlei**, on the left, and **Graslei**, on the right, comprise Ghent's oldest harbour, the **Tussen Bruggen** (Between the Bridges). This area was the commercial heart of the medieval city and the place where Ghent's guilds chose to build. If you wander about and spend enough time looking, you may be able to pick your favourite house, but the choice is not likely to be easy. Along Korenlei, ones to watch out for include: number 7, the 1739 **Gildehuis van de Onvrije Schippers** (House of the Tied Boatmen), an excellent example of Flemish baroque, with spectacular dolphins and lions adorning the gables and a gilded ship crowning the roof; and the 16th-century **De Zwane** (The Swans) at number 9, a former brewery that has a swan charmingly depicted in two carvings on the gables.

Look over the water to Graslei for a view of the even finer houses on that quay before crossing for a closer inspection. The **Gildehuis van de Vrije Schippers** (House of the Free Boatmen) was built in 1531, in Brabant Gothic style, while next door, the second baroque **Gildehuis van de Graanmeters** (House of the Grain Weighers) dates back to 1698. (Don't confuse this second grain weighers' house with the first one built up the road in 1435.)

The little **Tolhuisje** (Customs House), built in 1682, looks like a charming Renaissance afterthought. Next door is the Romanesque-style **Het Spijker**, also known as Koornstapelhuis (a former grain warehouse), dating from about 1200, and on the other side is the Korenmetershuis (Corn Measurer's house, now home to a restaurant), followed by the Gothic **Gildehuis van de Metselaars** (House of the Masons), dating to 1527 and built in Brabant Gothic style.

Korenlei's splendid guild houses

North of Korenlei

Jan Breydelstraat branches off from the north end of Korenlei. At number 5, occupying a house built in 1755 by the De Coninck family, is the **Design Museum Gent** (open Tues–Sun

10am–6pm; admission fee). Containing rooms decorated in period style, it is devoted to interior design and furnishings up to the 19th century, with a separate wing for modern furniture. Of historical note are pieces once owned by Catherine II of Russia and France's Louis XVIII (the French king, who was understandably nervous about Napoleon, fled to Ghent to avoid him).

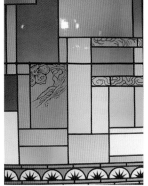

Stained glass by Constant Montald in the Design Museum Gent

The older wing contains a memorably ornate carved wooden rococo chandelier, while a room decorated in Empire style looks the most restful and harmonious. The new wing for modern furniture is an imaginative and exciting conversion of the old building, with internal balconies and gangways designed in an international style – it's rather like being on an ocean liner. Many of the modern items on display are equally innovative, including a curious armchair covered in quilted imitation banana skins.

Further along, in adjacent Burgstraat, the Renaissance-gabled house decorated with portraits of the Counts of Flanders (now a restaurant) is the **Huis der Gekroonde Hoofden** (House of the Crowned Heads).

Gravensteen

Turning right onto St Veerleplein leads to **Gravensteen**, the heavily renovated island fortress that was once the Castle of the Counts (open Apr–Sept daily 9am–6pm; Oct–Mar daily

9am–5pm; admission fee). The castle is still a powerful and ominous presence here, with massive fortifications comprising crenellated cylindrical towers and a vast brooding keep.

Work began on the structure in 1180 at the behest of Philip of Alsace, on the site of a 9th-century castle. The building was modelled on the Crusader castles of the Holy Land; a climb along the battlements (particularly at the top of the keep) provides excellent views and a welcome blast of fresh air. A tunnel leads to the central courtyard, which is surrounded by turreted walls. The central keep may be reached via a spiral staircase. Inside, the keep contains the living quarters of a succession of Counts of Flanders, including the impressive Great Hall where Philip the Good fêted the Knights of the Golden Fleece in 1445. An easy-to-follow, arrowed route takes you through the complex arrangement of narrow staircases, passages and chambers.

> **Children are usually wildly amused by Gravensteen's display of torture equipment, which includes a guillotine.**

From Kraanlei to Vrijdagmarkt

Between the castle and Kraanlei is Sint-Veerleplein, where the Inquisition burned its heretics on days when there wasn't a market. The old fish market at number 5 (with Neptune dominating the gateway) was constructed in 1689, in exuberant baroque style. Kraanlei is lined with various fine houses; at number 65 the almshouses are now home to **Het Huis van Alijn** (Alijn House; open Tues–Sun 11am–5pm; admission fee), the city's folklore museum. Built in 1363, this beautifully restored former children's hospital is comprised of 18 interconnected Flemish cottages arranged around a courtyard. Each room is decorated in the style typical of around 1900. The everyday life of working people is evoked through the items and tools they would have known and used and the few luxuries they could afford. The extensive display includes a variety of workshops and stores of the period, plus living and dining rooms.

Some other houses in Kraanlei that will draw your attention include numbers 1–13, built from the 14th to the 15th centuries. The 17th-century house at number 75, called 'De Klok', is decorated with allegorical designs representing such virtues as love, faith and justice. Numbers 77 and 79 are similarly covered.

Crossing the Leie via the Zuivelbrug leads to Grootkannonplein, where you will meet **Mad Meg** – not an eccentric Ghent citizen but a 16-ton cannon made in the 15th century. Standing on the quayside, supported by three stone plinths, it is quite harmless now and probably wasn't all that deadly when it was used, since early cannon were notoriously inac-

The folklore museum, in a former children's hospital

Ghent's oldest church, Sint-Jakobskerk (St James's) is east of Vrijdagmarkt, in a square of its own. Its structure is basically Romanesque but, as with so many others, the church's construction continued over several centuries, finishing in the 15th.

curate and this one cracked the first time it was fired.

Just a few steps away, **Vrijdagmarkt** (Friday Market) has some excellent examples of guild-houses, with a 19th-century monument to Ghent hero Jacob van Artevelde at the centre of the square. The stylish Art Nouveau building named **Ons Huis**, which was built in 1900, used to belong to the Socialist Workers' Association; it is attractive in itself, though too tall for the square. Older houses include those at numbers 22 and 43–47, built in the 17th and 18th centuries respectively.

It was in this square that the Flemish Counts were sworn in by the citizens of the city. Visible from the square in Koningstraat, the **Koninklijke Vlaamse Academie** (Royal Flemish Academy) is an imposing but rather badly worn baroque mansion that looms over the entire length of the street.

South of Vrijdagmarkt

A stroll from the church, a right turn into Belfortstraat and left at the Sint-Jorishof-Cour St George Hotel into Hoogpoort will take you to Nederpolder and the **Palais Vanden Meersche** at number 1. This house was built in 1547, but its lovely rococo courtyard (if you can catch a glimpse of it) was added in the 18th century. A total contrast in style is provided by the house opposite at number 2, a 13th-century Romanesque building called **De Kleine Sikkel**.

Turning right at the end of Nederpolder alongside the canal and Reep, you will see **Geraard de Duivelhof**, the turreted and fortified mansion that was constructed for the steward to the Flemish dukes, who was affectionately known as Geraard de Duivel (Gerard the Devil). Once used as an asylum for the mentally ill, the building, which has a Romanesque crypt, is now the home of the East Flanders State Archives.

You can follow the roads down to the confluence of the rivers Scheldt and Leie, crossing by way of Slachthuisbrug to see the ruins of **Sint-Baafsabdij** (St Bavo's Abbey; open Wed–Sun 9.30am–5pm; free). The abbey, which was founded in 630 by St Amandus, was once the most powerful in Flanders. Destruction, suppression and rebuilding

Going cheep: cage birds for sale at Vrijdagmarkt

over the centuries mean that today there is nothing much left of it, but parts of a cloister, the octagonal lavatorium (wash house for monks), the chapterhouse, and refectory can still be seen.

SOUTH OF SINT-BAAFSPLEIN

Some of the museums situated south of Sint-Baafsplein may be of interest only to specialists and devotees, and they go some way to justifying Belgium's reputation for being a nation of collectors. Even the museums that most people will wish to visit are not arranged as well as they might be, with some of the items randomly displayed and labelled in

Flemish only. Nevertheless, they have some marvellous exhibits that are well worth a look.

Around Veldstraat

Veldstraat, running south from Sint-Niklaaskerk, is the city's main shopping street, which you will soon realise from the crowds (the street is pedestrianised, but watch out for the trams). Many of the original building exteriors remain. The most historic and certainly the most flamboyant of these is the **Palais D'Hane-Steenhuyse**. The eye-catching rococo façade of this 18th-century house is matched only by the Classical façade of its garden frontage. Louis XVIII lived in the house briefly as he fled Napoleon; other inhabitants have included the French writer and statesman Talleyrand and members of the Russian royal family.

At number 82, the **Museum Arnold van der Haeghen** (open Mon–Fri 9.30am–noon and 2–4.30pm; free) is devoted to the library of Nobel Prize-winning writer Maurice Maeterlinck (1862–1949) and Ghent artist Victor Stuyvaert.

Ghent in Bloom

The Belgians are renowned for their green fingers and, as far back as the 16th century, plants were cultivated around Ghent in "orangeries" – ancestors of the modern greenhouse. Ghent's **Flower Festival** is held every five years in the city's Expo Halls (the next one is in April 2005). It's hard to believe that this enormous, sophisticated exhibition originated in 1809, when just 50 plants were displayed in a small inn rearranged for the occasion. Today, thousands of visitors admire glorious displays of ornamental flowers, fountains, gardens and the odd forest. Inspired by this abundance, the citizens of Ghent go to Kouter, a square which since the 18th century has hosted a flower and bird market every Sunday, to stock up on plants for their own gardens.

A riot of colour at the flower market held every Sunday at Kouter

The house was built in 1741; in 1815 it was home to the Duke of Wellington. It has a charming Chinese salon with silk wallpaper and some 18th- and 19th-century interior designs; it also hosts a variety of temporary exhibitions.

Turn left at Zonnestraat to **Kouter** and you will find yourself in a large square that has good claim to being the most historically significant one in the city. A variety of festivals, military parades, political demonstrations, meetings, archery contests and tournaments have taken place here through the centuries, and a flower market has been held in the square on Sundays since the 18th century. On an average Sunday, it unfailingly seems as if every tenth citizen is carrying a small tree here. It may be difficult to envisage all the pomp of the past, as very few buildings of any antiquity have survived; exceptions to this are the house at number 29 and the Opera House, situated just off the square in Schouwburgstraat, and completed in 1840.

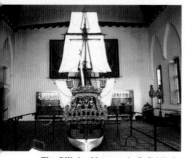

The Bijloke Museum's Guild Hall

The Bijloke Museum

Where Schouwburgstraat rejoins Veldstraat, turn into Nederkouter, which continues to parallel the Leie. Cross over where the signpost points the way to the **Bijloke Museum** (open Thur 10am–1pm and 2–6pm, Sun 2–6pm; free). Perhaps one of the main attractions of this museum is the building itself, which comprises a series of brick structures from the 14th to the 17th centuries that once formed the Cistercian convent of Bijloke. Arranged around a peaceful cloister, it is devoted to the arts of the Ghent region.

Despite a slightly flea-market approach to the organisation of its exhibits, it is well worth visiting for the interiors. Chief among these is the outstanding 14th-century refectory, painted in a warm terracotta, with a barrel-vaulted ceiling that measures over 31 m (100 ft) long and 14 m (45 ft) high.

The frescoes were painted in 1325 by an unknown master and include a faded but still beautiful *Last Supper*. Somewhat incongruously, the tomb of a 12th-century knight lies in the centre of the room. The Guild Hall, the original dormitory to the convent, is decked with splendid processional regalia of the Ghent guilds – banners, coats of arms and big ornamental lanterns, plus a model of a ship under full sail.

The Museum voor Schone Kunsten and SMAK

A 10-minute walk along Charles de Kerchovelaan leads to **Citadelpark**. In the eastern corner of the park (conveniently situated opposite the casino, if you're in the mood for a flutter) is the **Museum voor Schone Kunsten** (Museum of Fine

Arts; open Tues–Sun 10am–6pm; admission fee). Like the Bijloke Museum, the organisation of exhibits leaves something to be desired, but here too there are several very fine items on display. Bosch is represented by *Christ Carrying the Cross*, an unforgettable painting showing Christ on the way to Calvary. The artist emphasises the characters accompanying Jesus – a procession of grotesques. Even St Veronica, holding the cloth she used to wipe Christ's brow, seems more intent on her memento than the significance of the event itself. An earlier work, less characteristic of the artist, is *St Jerome at Prayer*, which also features the lion, a symbol of the saint and his conventional companion in portraits through the centuries. Good and evil are represented pictorially by different landscapes in the foreground and background.

Among other Flemish and Dutch exhibits are works by Jacob Jordaens, Frans Hals' bravura *Old Lady* – full of exuberant brushwork – and Pieter Brueghel the Younger's *Peasant Wedding* and a rather harassed *Village Advocate*. Rubens is represented by a *Scourging of Christ* (worth comparing with Lucas Cranach's painting on the same theme) and *St Francis Receiving the Stigmata*. Later paintings include works by Géricault, Corot, Courbet, Daumier, Ensor and Rouault. The Sint-Martens-Latem artists (whose 'colony' was near Ghent) are also represented. The museum has only a few sculptures, but there is a bust by Rodin and an erotic bronze by Camille Claudel.

Bosch's grotesque *Christ Carrying the Cross*

How Flanders Influenced Art

Medieval Flanders bequeathed some of the most profound and best-loved paintings to the world, the greatest of which can be seen in Bruges and Ghent. The brilliance of painters such as Bosch, Memling and Van Eyck sprang from the Gothic tradition that nurtured them. Gothic art was essentially a religious artform, with devotional paintings depicting the life of Christ, the Virgin Mary and the saints, but in Flanders it also came to place great emphasis on the accurate representation of the world, which was seen as God's creation and a vehicle for the sacred.

Van Eyck retained the religious subject matter of the Gothic tradition, but used the revolutionary medium of oil, enabling him to paint with greater control. No artist before him had observed nature so minutely, or was capable of rendering observations so precisely. His paintings (including his *Madonna with Canon George Van der Paele,* in Bruges, and the famous *Ghent Altarpiece,* in Sint-Baafskathedraal), along with those of Memling and artists such as Petrus Christus, Hugo van der Goes and Pieter Pourbus, reinforce this truthfulness to appearance.

The combination of sacred theme and faithful depiction of the world was taken a stage further a hundred years after Van Eyck in the work of Brueghel the Elder, whose paintings of biblical events are set in the recognisable peasant world of his time.

Nevertheless, the genius of an artist usually needs fertile soil in which to grow. For a long time the wealth of the Burgundian court and the merchant class of Bruges and Ghent was enough to pay for the commissioning of new works. Eventually, however, the economic centre of gravity moved northwards to Antwerp (home to Rubens and his pupil Van Dyck) and the Netherlands, where the first sophisticated market for genre paintings developed. Inevitably, the influence of Flemish painting moved with the money. Yet its preoccupations were to filter through the artistic world for centuries to come.

The permanent displays at SMAK (Stedelijk Museum voor Actuele Kunst, the Museum of Contemporary Art; open Tues–Sun 10am–6pm; admission fee) are mainly devoted to Belgian and international artists since 1945, with works on display by Bacon, Panamarenko, Broodthaers, Long and Nauman. In addition, the museum has rapidly established a reputation for its outstanding temporary exhibitions.

Sint-Pieterskerk's baroque dome can be seen from far around

Sint-Pietersplein

Northwards from the museum, Overpoortstraat leads to Sint-Pietersplein, where there are regular exhibitions of art and other cultural events at the **Kunsthal Sint-Pietersabdij** (St Peter's Abbey Arts Centre; open Tues–Sun 9am–5pm; admission fee). Situated next door, the **Schoolmuseum Michel Thiery** (Michel Thiery School Museum; open Mon–Fri 9am–5pm, Sun 2–5.30pm; admission fee) contains an eclectic mix of exhibits that relate to science taught in schools: fossils and stuffed animals sit cheek by jowl with minerals and model dinosaurs. The highly attractive museum building and courtyard (formerly the infirmary of St Peter's Abbey) have recently been fully restored, as was the adjoining church.

The splendid 57-m (188-ft) cupola of **Onze-Lieve-Vrouw Sint-Pieterskerk** (Church of Our Lady of St Peter) can be seen for many streets around. The baroque church was designed by the Huyssens brothers and built in 1719. Clearly, the architects were not lacking in ambition: the design is based on St Peter's Basilica in Rome. The impressive façade dominates attractive Sint-Pieterplein; the church has an exuberant baroque-style interior and artworks by Van Dyck. From Sint-Pietersplein, Sint-Kwintensberg leads to Nederkouter, and then Veldstraat.

TRIPS FROM GHENT

Ghent's central location, proximity to the capital, and extensive road and rail connections make it easy to get out and about to other places of interest. Most of those described here are no more than a few miles from the centre of the city. For descriptions of Brussels, Antwerp and Belgium's coastal resorts, see the *Berlitz Pocket Guide to Brussels* and the *Berlitz Pocket Guide to Belgium*.

Laarne Castle

Some 13 km (8 miles) east of Ghent, served by bus no. 688 from Sint-Pieters Station, **Kastel Laarne** (Laarne Castle; open Tues–Sun 10am–noon and 2–6pm; admission fee) is one of the best-preserved medieval moated fortresses in Belgium. Built in a pentagonal design in the 12th century as a defensive fortress for Ghent, it was added to in the 17th century.

The castle's towers, which have steeply pitched turrets, look as if they were made for a fairytale princess, while the remainder of the building, with its regularly spaced, mullioned windows, has the air of a substantial but comfortable manor house. A multi-arched bridge leads to a keep, beyond which are two central courtyards.

The rooms' furnishings are really magnificent, with most of the interiors in French and Antwerp style. There is splendid vaulting in the ground-floor hall and many exquisite chimneypieces. The most important furnishings are also the most beautiful: several 16th-century Brussels tapestries portraying the Emperor Maximilian on a hunt. There is also a gorgeous collection of French and Belgian silver from the 15th to the 18th centuries.

Sint-Martens-Latem and Deurle

These two villages on the banks of the Leie are respectively 8 km (5 miles) and 12 km (8 miles) southwest of Ghent. Both villages are picturesque in themselves, but are known chiefly for their connection with the Sint-Martens-Latem group of artists. There were, strictly speaking, two groups: one which formed around the sculptor George Minne in 1897, and an Expressionist group which formed in the 1920s after the interruption of World War I. The galleries and even the church in Sint-Martens-Latem have many of this second group's paintings on show. Deurle has three museums devoted to the work of Gust de Smet, his brother Leon de Smet, and to Flemish Expressionism as a whole.

Laarne Castle: one of the best preserved in Belgium

Ooidonk Castle

A little further southwest of Deurle, just 12 km (8 miles) from central Ghent, **Kasteel Ooidonk** (Ooidonk Castle) is situated in manicured gardens in a bend of the River Leie near the village of Bachte-Maria-Leerne. This startling château, with its Spanish-Flemish style of architecture, brings to mind St Basil's Cathedral in Moscow. A 16th-century building modernised in the 19th century, it stands almost as it did in 1595.

A ground-floor porticoed façade is echoed in a first-floor loggia, in turn surmounted by crow-stepped gables, steeply pitched roofs, turrets, chimneys and domed balconies. The moat's water laps around the massive circular towers. There is also a tavern, and the grounds of the castle extend into wooded parkland.

> Although Ooidonk Castle is still inhabited, by the Baron de Nevele, a splendid suite of apartments is sometimes open to visitors (Apr–June and Sept Sun only 2–5.30pm; July–Aug Sat and Sun 2–5.30pm; admission fee).

Oudenaarde

Only a 28-minute train ride from Ghent, the small town of Oudenaarde lies on the banks of the River Scheldt, 30 km (20 miles) to the south. Once famous for its thriving tapestry weaving industry, since the 18th century the town has, for the most part, fallen asleep economically. You can find a few restaurants in Stationsstraat, Hoogstraat and the Markt.

Undoubtedly, Oudenaarde's glory is the **Stadhuis**, located in the expansive Markt in the town centre. This 16th-century late-Gothic confection is the masterpiece of Brussels architect Henry van Pede. Dwarfing the buildings around the square, the town hall's yellow sandstone façade comprises a Gothic-arched portico, followed by two tiers of nobly proportioned windows, and topped with a wedding cake of a roof. The interior is open to visitors in the summer months.

In the square in front of the Stadhuis, the fountain of frolicking dolphins was financed by Louis XIV in 1671. Behind the Stadhuis is the 13th-century **Lakenhalle** (Cloth

Hall). **Sint-Walburgakerk** in the Markt has a leaning lantern-topped tower. Behind it is the **Notre Dame Hospital**, originally founded in the 12th century outside the town walls. There is a 13th-century chapel, though the main building dates from the 18th century. The **Bishop's residence**, dating from around 1600, is generally considered to be one of the finest Renaissance buildings in the country.

Stroll past the houses opposite the church and into the Burg, past the **Begijnhof** with its Renaissance archway. The Burg becomes Kasteelstraat before ending at the Scheldt. Across the river, the church of **Notre Dame of Pamele** is an early Gothic design of the 13th century. Up the road on the far side of the Tussenbruggen is the **Huis de Lalaing**, a pretty 1717 rococo house which has a museum and a workshop devoted to tapestries (a speciality of the town) and their restoration, together with an exhibition of work by local artists.

The exotic Spanish-Flemish architecture of Ooidonk Castle

WHAT TO DO

SHOPPING

The thought of shopping in Bruges or Ghent may not immediately leap to mind, but both cities have an excellent range of stores of all descriptions. Bruges is more adapted to the lucrative tourist trade than Ghent is, and you'll find more in the way of specialised stores and souvenirs. However, Ghent has the bigger shopping centre, with more of a 'city' ambience to it. Except for certain items, such as beer bought at the supermarket and chocolates, prices are probably what you would expect to pay at home.

Where to Shop

In Bruges, the main shopping street is Steenstraat, off the Markt, which has everything you would expect in the way of shops catering to everyday local needs, including clothes, shoes, food, home furnishings and electrical goods. There are also a few shops that sell Belgian chocolates and other souvenirs. The street and its associated malls become very crowded on Saturday, when the best time to go is first thing in the morning.

Bruges' network of small city-centre streets and alleys conceals a surprising number of shops, most of them specialising in items such as lace, chocolate or clothes. Particular streets to look

Shopping hours are from 9 or 9.30am to 5.30 or 6pm; many smaller shops close for an hour at lunchtime. Late-night shopping tends to be on Friday, with many stores staying open until 7 or 7.30pm. Shops that cater mainly to tourists (which in Bruges is just about all of them) usually open on Sunday.

Touring the main square

Tax-free shopping is available in stores that display the appropriate notice – usually the larger or more expensive specialised stores. If you're not sure, ask for details at customs or in the shop itself.

around are those surrounding the Burg and the Markt. Most of the city's squares have few shops: the Markt and the Burg are bounded by historical buildings with some cafés and restaurants; Jan van Eyckplein has none; and 't Zand is all bistros and hotels. The exception is Sint-Janplein, home of Bruges' theatre.

In Ghent, the main shopping street is Veldstraat, which is pedestrianised except for the trams, so do be careful and keep an ear open for the tram bell. The shops along this street are mostly for local consumption, but the streets and alleys leading off it conceal excellent specialist stores, as do Korte Meer, Voldersstraat and Niklaasstraat (parallel to Veldstraat). A modern shopping street, Lange Munt, links Hoogpoort with Vrijdagmarkt, which itself has only a few stores.

Both Bruges and Ghent have a number of markets. The main one in Bruges is on Wednesday on the Markt, and there is a bric-a-brac and craft market on 't Zand and Beursplain on Saturday (both open 7am–1pm). A giant flea market is held three times a year (in July, August and September) in Koning Albertpark and 't Zand. There's a flea market in Ghent at Bij St Jacobs and Beverhoutplein (Fri, Sat and Sun morning), and a daily flower market at Kouter (7am–1pm).

Good Buys

Antiques: These are plentiful in both Bruges and Ghent and are sold mostly in small, intimidatingly expensive-looking stores in the narrow side-streets off the main shopping areas.
Beer: This is a 'must buy' for connoisseurs, with many brands on sale that are simply not available at home. You

will need a car to carry significant quantities. The range of Belgian beers is vast, so it's safest to stick to those you have tried and liked rather than risk being disappointed by an unknown. Note that it is much cheaper to buy beer at conventional supermarkets, but they may not stock your favourites. A good place to try in Bruges is the Delicatessen Deldycke at Wollestraat 23, which stocks 'The Pride of Bruges' and 12-bottle selection crates.

In Ghent, the small shop in the Het Spijker building in Graslei provides presentation packs of a number of beers. You can buy Grain Genever (the gin speciality from Ghent) at Bruggeman, Wiedauwkaai 56.

Chocolate: 'Made in Belgium', undoubtedly the best in the world, is available everywhere. It's best to avoid the tourist-orientated products, such as the chocolate rabbits, and concentrate on the incomparable delights of the

Exquisite handmade chocolates are everywhere – and hard to resist

Handmade Belgian lace is easy to find – but expensive

classic, exquisite, hand-made Belgian praline and truffle. Selection boxes (pre-packed, or filled with your own choices) can be bought in a range of weights and are always gift-wrapped attractively. Prices vary hugely, with hotel-foyer stock the worst value for money. A good shop in Bruges is Van Oost at Wollestraat 9, a small store with a select range, while in Ghent, the Leonidas store in Veldstraat offers an exten-sive range at very reason-able prices. More exclusive and very much more expensive is the Godiva Chocolatier in Voldersstraat, which has a marvellous selection of beautifully presented and finely crafted chocolates.

Food and wine: Purchases may be limited by your appetite, the freshness of the produce, or even the size of your car, but it would be a shame not to come away with something, even if it's just for your return journey. Belgium is justly celebrat-ed for its pâtisseries and cakes, and there are some superb specialist food shops and delicatessens in both cities. Bruges is particularly well served: the picturesque De Trog Volkoren Bakkerij at Wijngaardstraat 17 has excellent fruitbreads and cakes. The Prestige Pâtisserie at Vlamingstraat 14 has an equally delectable selection, while the aforementioned Deli-catessen Deldycke at Wollestraat 23 has an excellent range of fine foods and wines. De Kaaskelder at Genthof 40 has racks of wine as well as gargantuan cheeses.

In Ghent, mustard made in the city can be bought from Tierenteyn at Groentenmarkt 3, and some delicious farm-made cheeses are available from Het Hinkelspel at F. Lousbergkaai 33.

Lace: Found everywhere in Bruges, but beware of imitations. Belgian handmade lace is expensive, but if you like lace this is the only sort worth buying. It should always be clearly labelled. Breidelstraat (connecting the Markt with the Burg) is the city's lace alley, but it really is sold throughout the city, so you'll have plenty of choice. Reliable sources of guaranteed, authentic Belgian handmade lace are the family-run Lace Jewel at Philipstockstraat 10–11 and Melissa at Katelijnestraat 38.

Lace is much less in evidence in Ghent, but a good, reliable source is Kloskanthuis at Korenlei 3.

ENTERTAINMENT

Walking, watching, eating and drinking are the chief pleasures of Bruges and Ghent, but you can tour the cities by boat and by horse-drawn carriage – peaceful and relaxing ways to see the sights (*see page 114–5*).

Café society is different in the two cities. Bruges' is more interior, since space and city preservation rules allow little else (although tables do appear outside in the summer, and some pedestrianised squares, like handsome little Huidenvettersplein, provide exceptions to this rule). In Ghent, given the right weather, outside eating is de rigueur and

Lunching *al fresco* in the Burg

there is more scope for *uitstappen* (strolling) and evening promenading. Belgium's 'beer culture' is polite, knowledgeable and often family-orientated (public drunkenness is rare), so it's quite safe for visitors to enjoy.

Bicycles are easy to rent *(see page 104)* and the cities are flat, though in Bruges you will have to cope with the cobblestones and in Ghent with the tram rails. From Bruges, you can cycle to Damme along the canal, while in Ghent you may like to visit the sights just outside the centre.

Nightlife

Music, opera, theatre: There are regular music festivals and concerts throughout the year in both cities: the city tourist offices will have the latest information. Bruges has performances of classical music, opera and dance at the

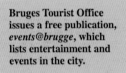

Concertgebouw, 't Zand, which opened in 2002, and at the Koninklijke Stadsschouwburg, Vlamingstraat 29. In Ghent, the Opera, Schouwburgstraat 3, is the

Bruges Tourist Office issues a free publication, *events@brugge*, which lists entertainment and events in the city.

most important concert and theatre address. Hotels and churches in both cities frequently host a variety of concerts and recitals.

Jazz, folk, rock: With its student population, Ghent is better served than Bruges, which tends to be quiet at night. The Cactus Club at Sint-Jakobsstraat 33 in Bruges is one of the most adventurous venues, with its electro-industrial and frontline-assembly bands, as well as nostalgia events like rock-and-roll dances.

In Ghent, a few desultory bars feature canned rock music, but the best place to go is the university area around Sint-Pietersplein and on Overpoortstraat where there is much more going on at night. The Lazy River Jazz Club at Stadhuissteeg 5 has live jazz every Friday evening, while the Damberd Jazzcafé at Korenmarkt 19 offers live jazz every Tuesday from October–March and every Monday in January and February. Blues music (of which the Belgians are fond) can crop up anywhere.

Cinemas: International films are usually shown in their original language, accompanied by subtitles. In Bruges, the weekly programmes are displayed in the tourist office; otherwise you can try the Kennedy in Zilverstraat, the Liberty in Kuipersstraat, and the Van Eyck in Smedenstraat. Ghent's most central cinema is the Sphinx in Sint-Michielshelling, but there is also the Decascoop in Ter Platen and the Studio Skoop in Sint-Annaplein.

Nightclubs and discos: There are virtually none and the few that do exist are not worth searching out unless you are truly desperate. In Ghent, most are to be found in the Zuid Quarter.

The Opera is Ghent's leading venue for theatre and classical music

SPORTS

Switch on any hotel television and you'll soon learn that football (soccer) is the top spectator sport (Bruges has its own soccer team, good enough to compete in Europe), while cycling and skating are also popular. In Bruges, information about all aspects of recreation can be supplied by Stedelijke Dienst Sport-Recreatie, tel: (050) 44 83 22, while in Ghent you can get information from Dienst Sport en Recreatie, Zuiderlaan 5, tel: (09) 243 88 90.

In both cities, you will find all sports facilities in the suburbs. In Bruges, there are swimming pools in Sint-Kruis and Sint-Andries; in Ghent, the Centre Blaarmeersen (see below) offers swimming, squash, tennis and athletics.

BRUGES AND GHENT FOR CHILDREN

Amusement parks: Boudewijnpark at A. De Baeckestraat 12, Bruges, includes a dolphinarium with daily shows throughout the year, fairground rides, a 'Holiday on Ice' show and Bambinoland, 'a paradise for the little ones' – tel: (050) 38 38 38. De Toverplaneet at Legeweg 88, is an indoor playground open Wed, Fri, Sat, Sun and public holidays.

By the lake in Ghent's Citadelpark

In Ghent, the Centre Blaarmeersen, a vast sports centre at Zuiderlaan 5, offers extensive footpaths and plenty of recreational opportunities for families, including cycling, roller-skating, swimming, mountainbiking and windsurfing, as well as camping – tel: (09) 243 88 70.

Museums and attractions: Most of the museums in Bruges and Ghent will only appeal to older children, but there are some exceptions. If they have heads for heights, children should love climbing the belfries in both of these cities. Gravensteen Castle in Ghent has lots of exciting towers, spiral staircases, battlements and dungeons, and there are some truly gruesome exhibits in the castle's torture museum. The Michel Thiery Museum in Ghent has dinosaur pictures and stuffed animals and fossils, as well as fluorescent minerals on display, all of which attract children of all ages.

All the fun of the fair at Boudewijnpark

Puppet theatre: The traditional puppet theatre is bound to enthuse younger children. In Ghent, the puppet theatre in the attic of Het Huis van Alijn (the folklore museum) occasionally holds performances. In both cities, tourist information offices have details of venues.

Tours: Apart from canal boat tours and horse-drawn carriage rides – both of which are popular with children – you can rent bicycles of sizes to suit the whole family and explore at the children's pace, or go on a coach tour of the surrounding countryside *(see pages 114–116)*. A trip to view the sand sculptures at Zeebrugge during August is an incentive to even the most expert sandcastle-builder.

Calendar of Events

For the most up-to-date information (specific dates, etc) on the festivals and arts calendar in either Bruges or Ghent, consult the relevant city's tourist office. The following list gives an idea of some of the major events taking place throughout the year.

March *Bruges:* Film Festival, held at various venues across the city.

April *Ghent:* Flower Festival, a magnificent international show hosted at the Flanders Expo centre every five years (next festival due in 2005).

May *Bruges:* Ascension Day Procession of the Holy Blood – an historical and ecclesiastical pageant. The *Dwars door Brugge* road race is also held in Bruges in May.

May–June *Ghent:* International Jazz Festival, with sessions staged at a variety of venues.

July–August *Bruges:* Zandfeesten, the largest flea market in Flanders (held on Sundays).

July *Ghent:* Ghent Festival – a range of musical and cultural festivities take place in the city centre.

Bruges: Cactus Festival – celebrating world music at Minnewater.

August *Bruges:* Festival of the Canals – a nocturnal pageant along the illuminated canals. Early Music Festival, various venues. Pageant of the Golden Tree – commemoration once every five years of the wedding of Charles the Bold and Margaret of York (next due in 2007).

Ghent: Patersholfeesten – various festivities in the Patershol area of the city. International Chamber Music Festival at various venues.

Zeebrugge: Sand Sculpture Festival – stunning transformation of part of the Zeebrugge seashore into towering works of art.

September *Ghent:* Flanders Festival – Ghent's share of the music festival, various venues.

October *Ghent:* International Film Festival.

November *Bruges:* International Antiques Fair.

December *Bruges:* Kerstmarkten, Christmas market and ice-rink at Markt and Christmas market at Simon Stevinplein. *Ghent:* Christmas market at Sint-Baafsplein.

EATING OUT

Belgians take their eating very seriously. Their cuisine is known around the world, and most of it is of excellent quality. Portions are generous; even if you ask for a sandwich, your plate will generally arrive loaded with much more than just garnish. Regional cuisines are strongly defined, but in the cities you should have no trouble sampling dishes from all over Belgium (and beyond).

Restaurants and Bars

Bruges and Ghent have a great many restaurants, cafés and bars from which to choose. The word 'restaurant' can mean anything from a formal, top-class establishment to a small café. Bars usually serve simple but hearty food at reasonable prices. Even in the smallest establishment you'll be served at your table so, if in doubt, simply take your seat: many waiters speak English and/or French.

Menus are often printed in a variety of languages, and at lunch (*middagmaal*) and dinner (*avondeten*) there is often a tourist menu and a choice of set menus at fixed prices; these are the best value. Some set meals are served only at lunchtime or only on particular days. Bars and cafés usually serve snacks in the morning and then lunch from around noon – times are posted in the window along with the menu. Many bars stay open until the early hours of the morning.

Many waiters speak English

Breakfast

Hotels serve substantial buffet breakfasts *(ontbijt)* which can see you through until lunchtime with no trouble at all. Along with tea or coffee and fruit juice, there will be a variety of breads, cheeses and cold meats, plus fresh fruit and cereal, yogurt and fruit salads, buns and pastries. You may be asked if you would like a boiled egg, and some hotels also provide buffet grills, so you can have a fried breakfast as well. Even in the smaller hotels the choice on offer is usually large and the food fresh.

Cold Dishes

A *boterham* is an open sandwich, which you'll find served just about everywhere. Usually comprising two or three huge slices of bread with the filling of your choice plus a salad, they are excellent accompanied by a Belgian beer – and offer great value. There is an enormous range, from salmon to meat to cheeses.

Fish and Shellfish

The close proximity of the North Sea and the traditional culture built around canal and river mean that fish dominates most menus. Alas, the canals of Ghent in particular are now virtually lifeless, but freshwater fish are brought to the table from further afield.

Sales tax and a service charges are nearly always included in the bill (service might not be), so there is usually no need to tip unless you want to. But it is customary to leave at least the small change.

One great favourite is fresh mussels *(mosselen)* in season (from Zeeland, in Holland), which are advertised everywhere when they are available, generally between mid-July and mid-February. Served simply with wedges of lemon, or

Dining out in Bruges offers something for every taste

cooked in a cream, white wine, or garlic and parsley sauce, they are a great delicacy and frequently arrive in a large pan from which diners help themselves. Mussels are best eaten with that other great Belgian staple, *frieten* (French fries).

Trout *(forel)* is another firm favourite, often served in a sauce of white wine, and eel *(aal or paling)* crops up on menus a lot, often served in thick sauces with herbs: *paling in 't groen* ('green eel') is boiled eel with green herbs. Fresh sole *(zeetong)* is mostly served grilled, while oysters, lobsters and crab are dressed in a variety of sauces. Many restaurants have a tank of lobsters or crabs on view to entice customers and prove the freshness of the dish.

The local coast delivers other seafood, such as herring, which are lightly salted on the boat and eaten raw as *maatjes*. Herring are also popular here and are delicious served smoked, steamed, marinated (Nieuwpoort) or in a rich, red wine sauce *(bonne femme)*.

Fish can also feature in the traditional *waterzooï*, a delicately flavoured stew made with vegetables and fish or chicken. *Waterzooï op Gentse wijze*, a dish orginating from Ghent, is also made with fish.

Meat and Poultry

Game, pork and beef play a prominent part in the Flemish diet, alongside chicken dishes such as *waterzooï*. *Carbonnade* is a classic Belgian dish of beef casseroled in beer, onions and herbs. There are steaks of fine quality, usually served with *frieten* (French fries).

Waterzooï is made with chicken (or fish) and a variety of vegetables

You may come across goose *(gans)*, boiled and then roasted. Veal *(kalf)* and liver *(lever)* dishes are also widely available. During the game season, rabbit or hare cooked in Gueuze beer with onions and prunes *(konijn met pruimen)* appears on menus, as well as rich pheasant dishes in thick sauces. *Wildzwijn* is wild boar.

Vegetables and Salads

You will find *witloof* (chicory) on most menus, served in a ham-and-cheese sauce; *stoemp,* a mixture of mashed potatoes and other vegetables, is often served with sausages.

Salad *(sla, salade)* is very much an incidental on Belgian menus, where meat and fish rule supreme. Salads to look out for include the *liégoise*, which contains green beans and potatoes and is served luke-warm, and the *wallonie*, which features a combination of potatoes and bacon.

Cheese

Cheese *(kaas)* comes in an enormous number of different types, most of them Belgian, Dutch or French. Belgium alone produces 300, including Trappist cheeses such as Orval and Chimay. Belgian Gouda and Remoudou are some of the more well-known names. Meals traditionally end with cheese, so leave some room for them if they are on the menu.

Desserts and Pâtisseries

Many restaurants offer English-language menus

The Belgians love a good dessert, and the more chocolate and cream it has the better. *Ijs* (ice cream) and *slagroom* (whipped cream) are usually involved somewhere, perhaps oozing from pancakes or waffles. The ideal way to round off a meal of mussels and *frieten* is with a *dame blanche* – vanilla ice cream and rich, hot chocolate sauce. The selection of cakes, fruit tarts, pastries, buns and biscuits available is immense.

Snacks

French fries are the staple snack of both cities, sold

from stalls and vans dotted around the streets. They can be topped with any one of a variety of calorie-laden sauces: ketchup, mayonnaise, mustard curry – you name it. There are fast-food places around town – in Bruges, they can be found mostly around the Markt, 't Zand and Steenstraat, and in Ghent you will see them in Vrijdagmarkt and the Veldstraat area.

Bars generally serve light snacks such as *Croque Monsieur* (toasted ham and cheese sandwich) and *Toast Cannibal* (toast topped with steak tartar), plus open sandwiches and filled rolls *(belegde broodje)*.

Vegetarians

Although the Belgian diet is dominated by fish and meat, it is easy to adhere to a varied vegetarian regime in Bruges and Ghent. However, this usually means foregoing traditional Flemish cooking. Listed in the Recommended Restaurants section *(see page 136)* are a number of places that serve vegetarian food. Be sure not to confuse vegetarian with *vleesgerecht*, which is a meat dish, and remember also that the Belgian French fry *(friet)* is likely to have been cooked in animal fat. Some 'vegetarian' restaurants also serve meat and fish. If you cannot find a specialist eating house, head for one of the many Italian restaurants – non-meat pasta dishes and salads are usually offered as a matter of course.

Drinks

Coffee *(koffie)* is fairly strong and usually served with extras such as little biscuits or chocolates, plus two or three kinds of sugar. Coffee liqueurs (especially Irish coffee) are popular and available everywhere. Tea *(thee)* is often served in a glass with lemon and without milk. Herbal teas are widely available.

Some of Belgium's many varieties of beer *(bier)* are described on page 100. Most bars stock at least 20 or 30, and a few will have more than 100. Those on tap *(van 't vat)* are cheaper than the bottled kind. All the usual spirits are available in generous measures. *Jenever* is the indigenous gin, and it is very strong. Most of the wine *(wijn)* is imported from France and Germany.

Essential bars to visit are (in Bruges) 't Brugs Beertje at Kemelstraat 5, where the friendly and knowledgeable landlord will advise you on all aspects of his 300 or so beers; De Garre, in the alley of the same name off Breidelstraat, which has a comfortable atmosphere and an impressive range of beers that includes its own brand; and (in Ghent) Het Waterhuis aan de Bierkant, Groentenmarkt 9, a popular canal-side bar with more than 100 beers; De Witte Leeuw, Graslei 6, a friendly bar with over 100 beers; and De Dulle Griet, Vrijdagmarkt 50, which has more than 250 types of beer, plus 1½-litre Kwak glasses on proud display.

Just a few of Belgium's hundreds of different – and excellent – beers

Hundreds of Brews

Beer is to the Belgians what wine is to the French and, indeed, many Belgian beers complete the last stage of their fermentation in corked bottles. Several hundred different sorts are produced, all of which have their distinctive character – and are served in their own type of glass.

Lambic beers are wild beers, so called because their fermentation involves exposure to wild yeast. Many have a sour, apple-like taste, but fruit may have been added to these to impart a distinctive flavour. *Kriek*, a delicious cherry beer, comes in a round glass (served hot if you wish to warm up), while *Frambozen* beer is a pale pink raspberry brew served in a tall stemmed glass. White beers are cloudy and generally light and youthful in flavour, like the *Brugse Tarwebier* drunk in Bruges.

The label *Trappist* refers to a large number of beers originally brewed in monasteries. *Tripel* denotes a very strong beer that was served to the abbot and other important personages; the monks drank the *Dubbel*, while the peasants (i.e. everyone else) had only a watery version. *Trappist Leffe* is a strong, dark beer, like Porter, slightly sweet and served in a bulbous glass.

Kwak (a strong, light-coloured beer) is served in a glass with a spherical base that sits in a wooden stand in order to remain upright. The 1½-litre glass and its stand are so valuable that customers must often give up a shoe to ensure they don't run off with the merchandise.

One of the strongest beers is the appropriately named *Delirium Tremens*, which can take you by surprise if you're not used to it – though if you see pink elephants, they are on the label and not in your head. Another powerful but delicious beer is *Corsendonck Agnus Dei*.

Other beers include *Gueuze*, a quaffable, honey-coloured, sweet variety served in a straight glass; *Loburg*, a Brussels-brewed light-coloured beer drunk from a vase-like receptacle; *Hoegaarden Grand Cru*, a coriander-based beer; *Rodenbach Grand Cru*, a red beer with a sharp apple taste; and *Bourgogne des Flandres*, a flavourful red beer.

To Help You Order ...

I'd like a/an/some ...

		Heeft u ...	
beer	**bier**	potatoes	**aardappelen**
bread	**brood**	salad	**sla, salade**
coffee	**koffie**	salt	**zout**
dessert	**nagerecht**	soup	**soep**
fish	**vis**	sugar	**suiker**
ice cream	**ijs**	tea	**thee**
meat	**vleesgerecht**	vegetables	**groenten**
milk	**melk**	water	**water**
pepper	**peper**	wine	**wijn**

... And Read the Menu

aardbei	strawberry	**mosselen**	mussels
appel	apple	**nieren**	kidneys
bonen	beans	**oesters**	oysters
boter	butter	**peer**	pear
eend	duck	**perzik**	peach
ei	egg	**pruim**	plum
garnalen	prawns	**ree**	venison
ham	ham	**rijst**	rice
haring	herring	**rode wijn**	red wine
honing	honey	**rund**	beef
jam	jam	**rodekool**	red cabbage
kaas	cheese	**sinaasappel**	orange
kers	cherry	**snoek**	pike
kip	chicken	**taart**	flan
koek	cake	**varken**	pork
kool	cabbage	**wit brood**	white bread
kreeft	lobster	**witte wijn**	white wine
lam	lamb	**worst**	sausage
macaroni	noodle	**zalm**	salmon

HANDY TRAVEL TIPS

An A–Z Summary of Practical Information

A

ACCOMMODATION (see also CAMPING, YOUTH HOSTELS, and the list of Recommended Hotels on page 129)

The tourist offices in Bruges and Ghent can provide detailed lists of hotels in each city that describe facilities, prices and contact details. They can also book rooms for you on payment of a deposit, which is then deducted from your hotel bill. If you arrive in either city without a room, try this service first.

In Bruges, contact Toerisme Brugge, Burg 8, 8000 Bruges, tel: (050) 44 86 86; fax (050) 44 86 00; e-mail <toerisme@brugge.be>; <www.brugge.be>.

In Ghent, contact Dienst Toerisme van Gent, Botermarkt 17a, 9000 Ghent, tel: (09) 266 52 32; fax (09) 225 62 88; e-mail <toerisme@ gent.be>; <www.gent.be>. The information desk is in the crypt of the Belfort.

Bruges is particularly busy in the summer months and at weekends, so it is advisable to book well in advance if you plan to visit at this time. If you are travelling in the low season or during the week, ask about discounts – many hotels do special deals from about October to March. The rates on page 129 are averages for double rooms in high season. Service charges and taxes are included. There is often a supplement for single rooms.

There is a star rating system (indicated in the tourist information literature and by the front door of the hotel), but the number of stars bears little relation to what you may get. Some four-star hotels may have certain facilities but still be unpleasant, while hotels further down the scale can be delightful. A few hotel exteriors and foyers look splendid, but this can be deceptive. Inspect rooms first if you can.

An extremely substantial breakfast is often included in the hotel rate. If you have to pay extra, do so, even if you're on a tight budget – it should be worth it, as it might enable you to skip lunch.

The Bruges tourist office also supplies a list of bed-and-breakfast accommodation in its brochure.

What's the rate per night	**Hoeveel kost het per nacht?**

AIRPORT *(luchthaven)*

Most flights into and out of Belgium use Brussels International Airport at Zaventem, 14 km (9 miles) from the centre of the capital, which is served by many major airlines. Following the demise of the Belgian national carrier Sabena in 2001, other airlines, including the new SN Brussels Airlines, have taken over many of its routes. The airport has all the facilities you would expect of an international airport.

There are train, bus and taxi connections from the airport to Brussels – the train links are the most efficient, running every half hour from the airport to all three of Brussels' main stations. From these there are regular train links to Bruges and Ghent. There are also some direct trains and special buses that connect Brussels Airport to Ghent.

The trip by taxi from the airport to the centre of Brussels will cost you substantially more than the train, but a reduction in the taxi fare is available if you present a round-trip air ticket. For flight information from within Belgium, tel: (0900) 70-000. The airport's website <www.brusselsairport.be> is also a good source of information.

B

BICYCLE HIRE (RENTAL)

Bruges encourages cyclists by allowing them to travel down more than 50 one-way streets in either direction (not as dangerous as it sounds because there are special cycle lanes). The Bruges Tourist Office issues a useful guide, *5 x Bike Around Bruges*. Bikes can be hired or loaned from many sources. Some hotels put bikes at their guests' disposal – ask when you arrive. They can be hired from the railway station in Bruges and Sint-Pietersstation in Ghent by the day. A discount is offered if you present a valid train ticket. In Ghent, tandems are also available. Bikes can be left at other participating rail stations – an information leaflet is available from stations and in advance from the Belgian tourist information office. Other hire locations in Bruges are 't Koffieboontje at Hallestraat 4 (tel: 050 33 80 27) and Fietsen Popelier at Mariastraat 26 (tel: 050 34 32 62).

| I'd like to hire a bicycle | **Ik zou graag een fiets huren.** |

BUDGETING FOR YOUR TRIP

Average, approximate prices in euros for basic items:

Airport transfer. Train from Brussels airport to Brussels Midi train station €3.

Bicycle hire. Generally from €7–9 per day, up to €18 a day for tandems.

Buses. Ghent–Bruges one-day pass €3.

Camping. €8–16 for a family of four for one night.

Car hire. €60–80 for a small car.

Entertainment. Cinema €7, ballet/opera tickets between €20 and €60, nightclub €8 upwards.

Guides and tours. Qualified guide €40 per 2 hours, €20 per additional hour; boat trip €6 (children half-price); horse-drawn carriage ride €25. Bruges: tourist office tour €4 (children free); 'Walkman' tour €8; city bus tour €10 (children €7); Quasimodo's Fun Tours including picnic lunch and entrance fees €40 (under 26 €30); organised cycling tours €20. Ghent: 'Discover Ghent' tour €50 per group (maximum 10 people); power boat hire €50 per 2 hours; organised pub crawl €15–20.

Hotels. Expensive from €150, medium €75–150, inexpensive €75 and below, for double room with bathroom and breakfast. (See RECOMMENDED HOTELS, page 129.)

Meals and drinks. Average prices for a reasonable meal, without drinks but including sales tax: breakfast €5–7, lunch from €10, dinner from €16, coffee around €2, beer €2–5, soft drink around €2. (*See Recommended Restaurants, page 136.*)

Museums Admission fees range from €1.50 for smaller museums to around €8 for major collections such as the Memlingmuseum in Bruges. Family tickets are available for all museums.

Shopping. Belgian handmade lace handkerchief around €10, Belgian chocolates per kilo €12–25.

Taxi. Meter charge €2.50 (€4.50 at night), plus €1.20 per km (€1.80 at night).

Trams. Flat-rate price for Ghent trams €1.

Trains. Return fares: Brussels–Bruges €20, Bruges–Ghent €10, Ghent–Brussels €12, Ghent–Oudenaarde €8.

Youth hostels. Bruges €8–12, Ghent €10–12, per person.

C

CAMPING

Belgium's campsites are graded from one to four stars and are usually excellently equipped. There are four recommended campsites in the vicinity of Bruges, which means you will have to find transport into the city centre. One of them, Camping Memling, also offers caravans and bungalows for rent and another, Kleinstrand, has chalets as well as tent pitches. The tourist information office provides details of all these campsites.

Camping in Ghent is largely confined to the four-star Blaarmeersen Sportcentrum and the one-star site at Witte Berken, details of which are also provided by the Ghent tourist office.

The Belgian tourist office will provide a camping leaflet on request. It is advisable to book pitches in advance during the high season. Spending the night in cars, caravans, mobile homes or tents by the roadside, in woods, dunes or directly on the beach is forbidden.

CAR HIRE *(autoverhuur;* See also D<small>RIVING</small> and B<small>UDGETING FOR</small> <small>YOUR</small> T<small>RIP</small>)

There are a lot of local car hire companies in both cities, so if time permits you should compare prices. Both tourist information offices provide information on car rental, and companies can also be found in the Yellow Pages telephone directory *(Gouden Gids)*. The minimum age can be 20 or 25, depending on the company and the vehicle. Credit cards are the preferred method of payment, and you will need to show your driving licence and passport (but never leave them with the hire company).

Many hotels have arrangements with car hire companies that make it simple to arrange for a car, but a small extra charge will normally be made for delivery to your hotel.

CLIMATE

Belgium has a temperate climate much influenced by its proximity to the sea, although obviously this influence diminishes inland. The warmest and driest weather is between April and October, but it can rain at any time of the year. Approximate monthly temperatures in Bruges and Ghent are as follows:

	J	F	M	A	M	J	J	A	S	O	N	D
°C	5	6	10	13	19	21	23	22	20	14	8	6
°F	41	43	50	55	66	70	74	72	68	57	46	41

CLOTHING

The unpredictable climate means you should be prepared for rain at any time of the year. A raincoat is advisable, but many hotels provide complimentary umbrellas. In March and April, the weather can be bright and reasonably warm, but with sudden blasts of cold wind as you turn a corner – so a light coat that can be slipped on and off is a good idea. In winter, heavy coats and pullovers are advisable. Bruges and Ghent are walking cities, so take comfortable, reliable shoes that you know will not hurt, and take care on the cobblestones.

Clothing is generally smartly relaxed and informal, but more expensive restaurants will expect male guests to wear ties.

COMMUNICATIONS (See also OPENING HOURS and TIME DIFFERENCES)

Post offices *(posterijen)*

The main post office in Bruges is at Markt 5. There are post offices in Ghent at Lange Kruisstraat 55 and Sint-Pietersstation. Opening times are Mon–Fri 9am–5pm, plus Sat mornings. Smaller post offices close for lunch from noon until 2pm. Mail boxes are red, often decorated with a white bugle. They are either free-standing or attached to walls. Stamps can also be purchased from souvenir shops and bookstores.

Faxes and telegrams

Most hotels have fax facilities; it is simplest to use these. Faxes and telegrams can also be sent during working hours from railway stations and post offices. Ghent has a telegram and telephone centre at Keizer Karelstraat 1.

Telephone

The phone system is reliable and extensive. Hotel phones are the most convenient, although they are also the most expensive. Public phone booths are plentiful, particularly in the city centres and railway stations; most of them can be used to phone direct overseas, and have instructions in English, French and German as well as Flemish. Many booths accept phone cards rather than coins: cards can be purchased from post offices, bookshops, newsstands and railway stations.

The dialling code for Belgium is 32; Brussels is 02, Bruges is 050, and Ghent is 09; you always need to use the local area code, even if you are calling from inside the area. Belgium has the usual telephone directories with white pages as well as a commercial Yellow Pages directory *(Gouden Gids)*, which has a useful English-language index.

E-mail

Many hotels offer e-mail facilities, and some will have data ports in the bedrooms. There is an Internet café, the Coffee Link, in Oud Sint-Jan at Mariastraat 38, Bruges, and a public e-mail and Internet facility at Bruges Online, Katelijnestraat 67, Bruges (cost €2 for 15 minutes). In Ghent, these facilities are found at The Globetrotter Internet Café at Kortrijksepoortstraat 180.

A stamp for this letter/ postcard, please.	**Een postzegel voor deze brief/briefkaart, alstublieft.**
airmail	**luchtpost**
registered	**aangetekend**

COMPLAINTS

If you have cause to complain, first speak to the relevant person on the spot, and then to the tourist information office or the police, depending on the nature of the complaint.

CRIME AND SAFETY (See also EMERGENCIES AND POLICE)

Its compactness and the numbers of tourists wandering its streets make Bruges extremely safe: you are seldom alone or far from the centre. There is very little crime, though obviously it makes sense to take elementary precautions with cameras, bags and personal effects. Valuables should be left in your hotel safe.

Ghent, also, is very safe, but it is wise to stay clear of the small red-light district between Keizer Karelstraat and Vlaanderenstraat, and the area around Sint-Pietersstation late at night.

If you are planning on venturing far into outlying areas of either city late at night, your hotel receptionist should be able to advise you on any areas best avoided.

CUSTOMS AND ENTRY REQUIREMENTS

Visitors from EU countries only need an identity card (or passport) to enter Belgium. Citizens of most other countries including the US, Canada, Australia and New Zealand must have a valid passport. European and North American residents are not subject to any health requirements. In case of doubt, check with Belgian representatives in your own country before departure.

As Belgium is a member of the European Union (EU), free exchange of non-duty-free goods for personal use is permitted between Belgium and the UK and Ireland.

Currency restrictions. There is no limit on the amount of euros or other currency that can be brought into or taken out of the country by non-residents.

D

DRIVING (See also CAR RENTAL)

To take your car into Belgium, you'll need:
• an international driving licence or your own licence (held for at least one year)
• car registration papers
• Green Card (this does not provide cover, but is internationally recognised proof that you have insurance – not obligatory for EU countries)
• a fire extinguisher and red warning triangle in case of breakdown
• a national identity sticker for your car
• headlight adaptors for right-hand-drive vehicles, to prevent the lights dazzling oncoming drivers

Driving conditions

Drive on the right, pass on the left. Though you may wish to drive to and from Bruges and Ghent, it is unnecessary and ill-advised to drive within the cities themselves. Bruges has a complex one-way system, with narrow winding roads that in high season are clogged with pedestrians, bicycles and horse-drawn carriages. Driving in Ghent is more aggressive than in Bruges and is made more complicated by the presence of trams, which you are not allowed to overtake and to which you must give way.

Belgium's motorway system is excellent, but it and the city ringroads (like that in Bruges) can get clogged at rush hour. Other main roads in Flanders are generally very straight and free of traffic – weekday travelling is very good indeed. Belgium's accident record is, however, one of the worst in Europe.

Rules of the road

Seat belts must be worn by both driver and passengers and there are stiff penalties for drink driving. Some offences require payment of fines on the spot.

An important rule to remember is that drivers should normally yield to traffic approaching from the right. A yellow diamond-shaped sign with a white border indicates that drivers on main roads have the right of way. When the sign reappears with a diagonal line through it, then drivers must yield to traffic from the right.

Speed limits

On motorways, the limit is 120 km/h (75 mph) and on other main roads it is 90 km/h (55 mph). In residential areas the speed limit drops to 50 km/h (30 mph). In all cases, lower limits may be indicated.

Parking

There is limited parking in the city centres. Larger car and coach parks exist around the perimeter of Bruges; it's safer (and quicker) to use them and walk into the centre. Both tourist offices provide maps indicating car parks.

Breakdown

Belgium's two main motoring organisations are the Touring Club de Belgique and the Royal Automobile Club de Belgique. They have reciprocal arrangements with other national motoring organisations. Motorways have emergency phones positioned at regular intervals.

Fuel and oil

Service stations are plentiful, and most international brands of petrol (gasoline) are on sale: leaded, unleaded *(loodvrij)* and diesel.

Road signs

International pictographs are widely used, but here are some written signs you may encounter:

Alle richtingen	All directions
Andere richtingen	Other directions
Beschadigd wegdek	Bad road surface
Doorgand verkeer	Through traffic
Eenrichtingverkeer	One-way street
Langzaam rijden	Slow
Moeilijke doorgang	Obstruction ahead
Opgelet!	Caution!
Tol	Toll
Wegomlegging	Detour
Zachte berm	Soft shoulder

Are we on the right road for …?	**Zijn wij op de juiste weg naar …?**
Fill the tank, please.	**Vol, graag.**
Check the oil/tyres/battery.	**Kijkt u even de olie/banden/accu na.**
I've broken down.	**Ik heb autopech.**

E

ELECTRICITY

Belgium operates on 220 volts, 50 Hz AC, requiring standard two-pin round continental plugs. Visitors should bring their own adapters.

EMBASSIES AND CONSULATES *(ambassades; consulaten)*

Australia: rue Guimard 6–8, 1040 Brussels, tel: (02) 286 05 00
Canada: avenue de Tervuren 2, 1040 Brussels, tel: (02) 741 06 11
Ireland: rue Wiertz 50, 1040 Brussels, tel: (02) 235 66 76
New Zealand: Square de Meeûs 1, 1000 Brussels, tel: (02) 510 12 40
South Africa: (consulate): rue de la Loi 26, 1040 Brussels,
tel: (02) 285 44 00
UK: rue d'Arlon 85, 1000 Brussels, tel: (02) 287 62 11
US: boulevard du Régent 27, 1000 Brussels, tel: (02) 508 21 11

EMERGENCIES *(noodgeval;* See also MEDICAL CARE and POLICE)

The three-digit emergency telephone numbers listed below are valid throughout Belgium:

Emergency/police	101
Accidents	112
Fire brigade/ambulance	100

I need a doctor/dentist.	**Ik heb een arts/tandarts nodig.**
hospital	**ziekenhuis**

ENVIRONMENTAL ISSUES

You may be tempted to buy exotic souvenirs from shops selling African artefacts, but spare a thought for endangered plants and animals which might be threatened by this trade. What you buy may be illegal and your souvenirs could be confiscated by Customs on your return home. For further information, contact the following:

UK: HM Customs & Excise, tel: (0845) 010 9000; (44) 20-8929 0152 from outside of the UK.

US: Fish and Wildlife Service, tel: (703) 358 2095; fax: (703) 358 2281.

ETIQUETTE (See also TIPPING)

The citizens of Bruges and Ghent are open, friendly and patient. Most will say that they speak only a little English, then go on to speak it fluently. However, do not assume that everyone will speak English. The great majority of bars, cafés and restaurants permit smoking, often in designated areas.

G

GAY AND LESBIAN TRAVELLERS

The Federatie Werkgroepen Homoseksualiteit, Vlaanderenstraat 22, 9000 Ghent is Belgium's largest gay and lesbian organisation. Information hotline, tel: (09) 238 2626; e-mail <fwh@innet.be>. The age of consent for gay men is 16.

GUIDES AND TOURS (gids; tolk; See also BUDGETING FOR YOUR TRIP)

Bruges

Guided tours allow you to explore parts of the city that you might not discover on your own. Groups and individuals can book qualified guides in advance from the tourist office, for a tour of two-hour (minimum) duration. During July and August there are daily guided tours of the city, starting at 3pm from the tourist office. 'Walkman' tours, which are suitable for two people at a time, are available from the tourist office.

Bruges's canals can be explored 10am–6pm daily in summer (only weekends and holidays in winter). Boats depart from Rozenhoedkaai, Dijver and Mariastraat. Night tours for groups can also be arranged on request. It can be chilly on these tour boats, and even on a warm summer day you may be grateful for a sweater or jacket.

A 50-minute tour round Bruges by bus with taped commentary in the language of your choice is operated by Sightseeing Line, tel: (050) 35 50 24, with minibuses departing from the Markt at regular intervals. The same line operates tours to Damme for different durations, depending on the season: they also depart from the Markt and can include a free drink and pancake in Damme, and a return canal trip on the Lamme Goedzak paddle-boat.

Quasimodo's Fun Tours (tel: 0800 97 525) run minibus tours of the countryside and Flanders Fields, including a beer-themed itinerary.

Horse-drawn carriage rides through the city centre depart from the Markt (occasionally from the Burg), with a 10-minute break for the horse at Minnewater. Commentary is provided by the driver.

Cycling tours in and around Bruges (following minor roads) include provision of a mountain bike, guide, transport by bus, insurance and rain gear; tel: (050) 33 07 75.

Ghent
The tourist office provides details of qualified guides for tours of minimum two-hour duration. A *Discover Ghent* guide includes a qualified guide, boat excursion and visit to the Belfort.

Guided tours (in various languages) by boat through the city-centre canals last 45 minutes: boats depart from Korenlei and Graslei. Scheduled boat trips to Bruges and Ooidonk are also available in summer from Benelux Rederij, Recolletenlei 32, tel: (09) 225 15 05. You can rent four- and five-seater electrically powered boats: minimum age 16; reserve in advance from Rederij Minerva, Kareelstraat 6, tel: (09) 233 79 17.

A group pub crawl involving a boat tour and walk with the town crier can be arranged: information and reservations are available from Orde van de Belleman, Rozemarijnstraat 23, tel: (09) 220 48 02.

From Easter until the end of October, every day between 10am and

6pm, a 30-minute horse-drawn carriage ride through the city departs from Sint-Baafsplein.

L

LANGUAGE

About 60 percent of the population living in Flanders – which covers roughly the northern half of Belgium – speak Flemish (Dutch with a different accent from that spoken in Holland). French is the language in Wallonia, southern Belgium, and a small percentage of the people in the eastern districts of the country speak German as their first language.

English is spoken by many and should be at least partially understood by virtually everybody. Written and spoken Flemish is sometimes extremely similar to English; at other times there are no clues as to meaning. Menus may be printed in English as well as Flemish and French; if they are not, most staff will be happy to explain what things are.

Although local road signs are in Flemish, be aware that many towns bear different names in French. Brugge (Flemish) is *Bruges* in French; Gent/*Gand*; Ieper/*Ypres*; Oudenaarde/*Audenarde*; Antwerpen/*Anvers*.

Good morning	**Goede morgen**
Good afternoon	**Goede middag (or Goedenamiddag)**
Good evening	**Goedenavond**
Goodbye	**Dag/tot ziens**
today	**vandaag**
yesterday/tomorrow	**gisteren/morgen**
day/week	**dag/week**
month/year	**maand/jaar**
left/right	**links/rechts**
cheap/expensive	**goedkoop/duur**
hot/cold	**warm/koud**

Days and Months

Sunday	**Zondag**	January	**Januari**
Monday	**Maandag**	February	**Februari**
Tuesday	**Dinsdag**	March	**Maart**
Wednesday	**Woensdag**	April	**April**
Thursday	**Donderdag**	May	**Mei**
Friday	**Vrijdag**	June	**Juni**
Saturday	**Zaterdag**	July	**Juli**
		August	**Augustus**
		September	**September**
		October	**Oktober**
		November	**November**
		December	**December**

Numbers

0	**nul**	16	**zestien**
1	**een**	17	**zeventien**
2	**twee**	18	**achttien**
3	**drie**	19	**negentien**
4	**vier**	20	**twintig**
5	**vijf**	21	**een en twintig**
6	**zes**	30	**dertig**
7	**zeven**	40	**veertig**
8	**acht**	50	**vijftig**
9	**negen**	60	**zestig**
10	**tien**	70	**zeventig**
11	**elf**	80	**tachtig**
12	**twaalf**	90	**negentig**
13	**dertien**	100	**honderd**
14	**veertien**	200	**tweehonderd**
15	**vijftien**	1,000	**duizend**

LAUNDRY AND DRY CLEANING *(wasserij; stomerij)*

The large hotels offer same-day or next-day service, but not on weekends and holidays – and it's expensive. Dry cleaners and launderettes are cheaper, but they are mainly located in outer residential areas.

When will it be ready?	**Wanneer is het klaar?**
I must have it for tomorrow morning.	**Ik heb dit morgenvroeg nodig.**

LOST PROPERTY

It is best to first contact the police. In Bruges, the central police station is at Hauwerstraat 7, tel: (050) 44 88 44. In Ghent, contact the city centre police station at Belfortstraat 4, tel: (09) 266 61 30. Taxi drivers usually hand things to their head office or to the police.

I've lost my ...	**Ik ben mijn ... kwijt.**
handbag	**handtas**
passport	**paspoort**

M

MEDIA

Newspapers and magazines *(kranten; tijdschriften)*

The best places to look for English-language publications are at the railway station kiosks and larger bookshops and newsstands. Larger hotels often stock the *International Herald Tribune*, the *Financial Times* and other quality international newspapers.

Radio and television

BBC long-wave and world services and European-based American networks can be picked up easily. Most hotels have cable television with up to 30 channels, including BBC World from the UK and CNN International from the US. Many European channels show English-language films and programmes with subtitles.

> Have you any English newspapers? **Heeft u Engelse kranten?**

MEDICAL CARE (See also EMERGENCIES)

Travellers from EU countries should receive free medical treatment in Belgium. For citizens of the UK this means presenting an E111 form, which can be obtained from the post office – if you are still charged for treatment and drugs, you will have to seek reimbursement from the UK Department of Health. However, it is wise to take out extra travel insurance, which should cover illness, accident and lost luggage. For non-EU citizens, travel insurance is essential.

A Belgian pharmacy *(apotheek)* is identified by a green cross and should have a list in the window of nearby late-night chemist shops. Such lists are also published in the local weekend press.

Call police or tourist information office for telephone number of doctors on weekend and night duty.

> Where's the duty pharmacy? **Waar is de dienstdoende apotheek?**

MONEY MATTERS

Currency

The unit of currency in Belgium is the euro, which is abbreviated to € and divided into 100 cents. Coins are: €2, €1, and 50, 20, 10, 5, 2 and 1 cents. Banknotes are: €500, 200, 100, 50, 20 10 and 5.

Exchange facilities

There is a standard commission for changing foreign currency and travellers' cheques. Generally, banks offer the best rates, followed by bureaux de change. Hotels often exchange currency at an inferior rate. Currency-exchange machines at Brussels Airport make transactions in several currencies. ATMS accepting non-Belgian debit and credit cards are widely available.

Credit cards *(credit card)*

Major hotels and many restaurants and shops accept payment by international credit cards.

Travellers' cheques *(reischeque)*

These are widely accepted and can be cashed as long as you have your passport with you.

Sales tax, service charge

Called BTW, a sales (value-added) tax is imposed on most goods and services. In hotels and most restaurants, this is accompanied by a service charge. Both are included in the bill. To recover some of the tax on expensive purchases, look for shops displaying the signs 'Europe Tax-Free Shopping' or 'Tax-Free International'; retailers are well acquainted with the necessary procedures.

I want to change some pounds/dollars.	**Ik wil graag ponden/dollars wisselen.**
Do you accept travellers' cheques?	**Accepteert u reischeques?**
Can I pay with this credit card?	**Kan ik met deze credit card betalen?**

O

OPENING HOURS (See also PUBLIC HOLIDAYS)

Banks open Mon–Fri 9am–noon, 2–4pm and some until 5pm. Some

banks open on Saturday morning and until 6pm on one or two days per week. Shops and department stores are generally open Mon–Sat 9am–5.30pm or 10am–6pm. Many smaller shops close for an hour for lunch. Late-night shopping is on Friday until 7pm. Many stores are closed on Sunday. Post offices are open Mon–Fri 9.30am–12.30pm, and 2–5pm. Larger post offices are also open Sat 9am–noon.

Museums are generally open Tuesday to Sunday from 9.30 or 10am to 5pm, but the smaller ones often close for an hour for lunch. In Bruges, some may be closed on Tuesday or Wednesday during the low season.

P

PHOTOGRAPHY AND VIDEO

All makes of film and equipment are widely available, as is one-hour processing.

I'd like a film for this camera.	**Mag ik een film voor dit toestel.**
How long will it take to develop this film?	**Hoe lang duurt het ontwikkelen van deze film?**

POLICE (See also EMERGENCIES)

The *politie* can be reached on the emergency 101 phone number. They are not that much in evidence on the streets (there is seldom any need for them), but they are usually dressed in dark blue. Any theft should be reported at the nearest police station.

Where's the nearest police station?	**War is het dichtsbijzijnd politiebureau?**

PUBLIC HOLIDAYS *(openbare feestdagen)*

Most shops are closed on public holidays; if museums are not closed, they will be operating on Sunday hours. If a holiday falls on a Sunday, the following Monday will usually be taken off instead.

1 January	*Nieuwjaar*	New Year's Day
1 May	*Dag van de Arbeid*	Labour Day
21 July	*Nationalefeestdag*	National Day
15 August	*Maria Hemelvaart*	Assumption
1 November	*Allerheiligen*	All Saints' Day
11 November	*Wapenstilstand*	Armistice Day
25 December	*Kerstdag*	Christmas Day
Moveable dates:	*Paasmaandag*	Easter Monday
	Hemelvaartsdag	Ascension Day
	Pinkstermaandag	Whit Monday

R

RELIGION

The population of Belgium is predominantly Roman Catholic, but Protestant churches are also well represented in both cities. In Bruges, there is an English church at Keersstraat 1 and an Ecumenical chapel at Ezelstraat 83.

T

TIME DIFFERENCES

The following chart shows the time difference between Belgium and various cities in winter. Between the beginning of April and the end of October Belgian clocks are put forward one hour.

New York	London	**Belgium**	Jo'burg	Sydney	Auckland
6am	11am	**noon**	1pm	10pm	midnight

TIPPING

In a country where service is included in most bills, tipping is not a problem. Most people will not expect a tip (but will still appreciate one). Possible exceptions are public toilets, where the attendant may expect a tip of 25–50 cents, and porter and maid service in the more expensive hotels.

TOURIST INFORMATION OFFICES

United Kingdom: Tourism Flanders-Brussels, 31 Pepper Street, London E14 9RW, tel: (0900) 188 77 99 (calls cost 60p per minute); fax: (020) 7458 0045; e-mail: <info@flanders-tourism.org>; <www.visitflanders.com>.

US: Belgian Tourist Office, 780 Third Avenue, Suite 1501, New York, NY 10017, tel: (212) 758 8130; fax: (212) 355 7675; <www.visitbelgium.com>.

The information office in Bruges is in the Burg, tel: (050) 44 86 86; fax: (050) 44 86 00; e-mail: <toerisme@brugge.be>; <www.brugge.be>, open daily 10am–1pm and 1.30–6pm during the summer, 9.30am–5pm in the winter. There is also a tourist information office at the railway station, from where you can book hotel accommodation in the city.

The free monthly newsletter, *Exit*, and brochure, *events@brugge*, are available in English from the tourist offices, which also offer a free monthly newspaper, *Brugge Cultuurmagazine*. It is in Flemish, but performance dates and venue details are fairly easy to understand.

In Ghent, the information office is in the crypt of the Belfort in Botermarkt, tel: (09) 266 52 32; fax: (09) 225 62 88; e-mail: <toerisme@gent.be>; <www.gent.be>. It is open during the summer Mon–Fri 9.30am–6.30pm; Sat, Sun, and public holidays 10am–noon and 2pm–6.30pm. In the winter, Mon–Fri 9.30am–5pm; Sat and Sun 9.30am–1pm.

Where is the tourist office?　　**Waar is het toeristen-bureau?**

TRANSPORT (See also BUDGETING FOR YOUR TRIP)

In cities where everything seems to be a short walk away, public transport is not usually a problem.

Buses

In Bruges, buses to the suburbs can be caught most conveniently in the Markt or at the train station. Sightseeing buses and excursions also depart from the Markt. Other main bus stops are at Wollestraat, Biekorf and Kuipersstraat. A one-day pass allows unlimited travel on all the city's buses. Regional buses (to destinations outside Bruges) can be caught at the train station and in 't Zand. A helpline is available for both types of bus on (070) 22 02 00, and schedules are also displayed in the tourist information office.

In Ghent, the main bus station is outside Sint-Pieters train station. This is also a terminus for many of the city's trams, which serve most of Ghent and are great fun to ride. Buses and trams can also be caught from the city centre, at Korenmarkt.

Taxis

Taxis are plentiful in Bruges and Ghent, where they flock together outside the train stations for the hotel run. Order your taxi at the hotel when you check out, and one will arrive in two or three minutes. However, taxis are rather more difficult to hail in the streets – in Bruges, you are most likely to find one in the Markt, while in Ghent, the best place to try hailing a taxi is Korenmarkt.

Trains

The Belgian railway network is superb. Bruges and Ghent are situated on the same line that connects Brussels with Ostend. Train services are prompt and frequent. Announcements on inter-city trains are given in Flemish, French and English, and text-screen panels in each carriage give the name of the next station. Information and assistance are available at both cities' train stations.

There are first- and second-class carriages and smoking and non-smoking sections (smoking carriages are likely to be phased out soon). A range of discounts are offered at weekends and on long-term passes.

When is the next bus/ train to…?	**Wanneer vertrekt de volgende bus/trein naar…?**
I want a ticket to…	**Ik wil graag een kaart naar…**
one way (single)	**enkele reis**
round-trip (return)	**retour**
first/second class	**eerste/tweede klas**

TRAVELLERS WITH DISABILITIES

Facilities and accessibility to transport and buildings in both cities are distinctly patchy. The cobblestone streets and medieval buildings of Bruges mean access to places of interest can be challenging, particularly as ramps and railings are invariably absent. Some hotels have ramps, but planning rules for older hotels forbid the installation of lifts, so all or some of the rooms can only be reached by the staircase. Museums are often similarly restricted, and may involve many stairs. The picture is much the same in Ghent.

Some of the larger (chain) hotels have specially designed rooms for guests with disabilities *(see Recommended Hotels on page 129)*. There are, at most, usually two or three such rooms per hotel:

No public transport is equipped with lifts or ramps, and train carriages are frequently so high off the ground that one could do with a rope ladder, but assistance is available at railway stations.

At some major road crossings in both cities, textured soft paving has been installed. All travellers should be careful near the canals, which often are not railed off from the footpath or road.

Tourist information offices should be able to provide literature on those facilities that are available; Bruges tourist information produces a map showing free parking facilities for drivers with disabilities.

In the UK, information for travellers with disabilities may be obtained from Holiday Care, tel: (01293) 774535; fax: (01293) 784647; <www.holidaycare.org.uk>, or from RADAR, Unit 12, City Forum, 250 City Road, London EC1V 8AF, tel: (020) 7250 3222; <www.radar.org.uk>.

In the US, contact the Society for the Advancement of Travel for the Handicapped (SATH), 347 Fifth Avenue, Suite 610, New York, NY 10016, tel: (212) 447 7284; fax: (212) 725 8253; <www.sath.org>.

TRAVELLING TO BRUGES AND GHENT

By air

Brussels Airport *(see page 104)* is linked by direct flights with major airlines from all European and many North American cities, but other long-distance travellers may have to connect via Amsterdam, London or Paris. There are no charter flights.

By coach

Many coaching holidays and direct long-distance bus services to Bruges and Ghent are available from European capitals (including London) and provincial cities.

By rail

Brussels, Bruges and Ghent have excellent rail connections with the rest of the European network. There are various discounts for EU residents, and it's best to contact your local rail operator for the latest information before your trip.

From the UK it's possible to reach Bruges and Ghent easily using the excellent Eurostar service through the Channel Tunnel. Trains depart from Waterloo International in London or Ashford International in Kent and arrive in Brussels within three hours. You can be in Bruges or Ghent in just over four hours. Check-in time at Waterloo International is just 20 minutes before departure (and is strictly applied, so make sure you arrive on time), and your bags are with you at all times, so there is no delay waiting for luggage once you arrive. Trains are comfortable, and pay phones are located in every carriage. Any passport controls are at your final destination only.

Seats should be reserved well in advance: this can be done direct (tel: 08705 186186; <www.eurostar.com>) or at some mainline stations and travel agents. If you do travel by Eurostar to Brussels and book your hotel through Belgian Tourist Reservations (tel: +32 2 513 74 84), you may be entitled to a discount on your accommodation in Bruges and Ghent.

If you want to take your car, Le Shuttle trains travel via the Channel between Folkestone and Calais every 15 minutes. Passengers stay with their car for the 35-minute journey. Tel: (08705) 353535; <www.eurotunnel.com>.

By sea

P&O Ferries, tel: (08705) 202020; <www.poferries.com> operates an overnight car ferry service from Hull to Zeebrugge.

Once every two days, Superfast Ferries, tel: (08702) 340870; Belgium <www.superfast.com> operates an overnight car ferry service from Rosyth (Edinburgh) to Zeebrugge.

Hoverspeed (tel: 0130 486 5000; <www.hoverspeed.com>) has multiple daily high-speed Seacat services operating between Dover and Calais.

W

WATER

It is perfectly safe to drink tap water in Belgium.

WEBSITES

General information can be found at <www.visitbelgium.com> and <www. visitflanders.com>. The tourist boards for both cities operate websites, <www.brugge.be> and <www.gent.be>. Useful sites for planning your travel arrangements are <www.b-rail.be> and <www.brusselsairport. be>. In addition, many of the hotels have their own websites *(see Recommended Hotels, page 129).*

WEIGHTS AND MEASURES

Like most of Europe, Belgium uses the metric system.

1 metre	=	approx 39 ins
1 kilometre	=	1,093 yards or approx 0.6 mile
16 km	=	approx 10 miles
1 kilogram	=	approx 2.2 lb
1 litre	=	1.75 pints
40 litres	=	approx 9 gallons (10 US gallons)

WOMEN TRAVELLERS

Women can wander anywhere in Bruges and Ghent without being subjected to sexual harassment. Avoid the red-light area of Ghent, between Keizer Karelstraat and Vlaanderenstraat.

Y

YOUTH HOSTELS

Bruges and its immediate neighbourhood have a number of 'Youth Hotels' and Youth Hostels. There are three located in the city itself, notably: Bauhaus International Youth Hotel, Langestraat 135–137, tel: (050) 34 10 93; fax (050) 33 41 80; e-mail <info@bauhaus.be>; <www.bauhaus.be>; The Passage, Dweersstraat 26, 800 Bruges, tel: (050) 34 02 32; fax: (050) 34 01 40; and Snuffel Sleep-in, Ezelstraat 47–49, tel: (050) 33 31 33; fax: (050) 33 32 50; e-mail: <info@ snuffel.be>; <www.snuffel.be>.

The attractive and well-equipped Youth Hostel in central Ghent is: De Draecke, Sint-Widostraat 11 (Gravensteen), 9000 Ghent, tel: (09) 233 70 50; fax: (09) 233 80 01; e-mail <youthhostel.gent@skynet.be>.

Recommended Hotels

With more than 100 hotels throughout the city, Bruges presents more choice as to establishment and location, while Ghent's hotels tend to cluster in the city centre and around the station. Like everywhere else, hotels that are part of an international chain will provide a predictable degree of comfort, but guests may miss out on more authentic Flemish hospitality provided by locally run establishments. Both tourist information offices provide brochures listing hotels. It's always advisable to book in advance. Bruges is particularly crowded in the summer, tending to be busiest at weekends. Ghent is less crowded, but still busy, and has far fewer hotels.

Prices are based on the cost per night of a double room with en suite bath or shower, including service charge, sales tax and breakfast. Rates can vary according to the season or time of week. All the hotels listed here accept major credit cards.

€	below 75 euros
€€	75–150 euros
€€€	above 150 euros

BRUGES

Acacia €€ *Korte Zilverstraat 3A–5, 8000 Bruges, tel: (050) 34 44 11; fax: (050) 33 88 17; <www.hotel-acacia.com>.* This comfortable modern hotel (part of the Best Western chain) is centrally located just off the Markt. All rooms have private bathroom, television, kitchenette, minibar, radio, telephone and safe. Health club, swimming pool, solarium. Underground parking. 48 rooms.

Azalea €€ *Wulfhagestraat 43, 8000 Bruges, tel: (050) 33 14 78; fax: (050) 33 97 00; <www.azaleahotel.be>.* Family-run hotel in a 14th-century house on the banks of the Speelmansrei canal, 200 m (250 yards) from the Markt. Comfortably furnished, with a lovely Art Nouveau staircase. 25 rooms.

Bourgoensche Cruyce €€€ *Wollestraat 41–43, 8000 Bruges, tel: (050) 33 79 26; fax: (050) 34 19 68; e-mail: <bour.cruyce@ ssi.be>; <www.brugge.be>*. Tiny, charming wooden-fronted hotel in a superb canalside location. All rooms are very well furnished, antiques and old books abound, and the hotel has a renowned gastronomic restaurant *(see page 136)*. 5 rooms.

Cavalier € *Kuipersstraat 25, 8000 Bruges, tel: (050) 33 02 07; fax: (050) 34 71 99; <www.users.skynet.be/hotel.cavalier>*. In spite of its slightly ramshackle external appearance, this small hotel is friendly and ordered and provides good value for the cheaper range of hotels. 8 rooms.

Crowne Plaza Bruges €€€ *Burg 10, 8000 Bruges, tel: (050) 44 68 44; fax: (050) 44 68 68; <www.crowneplaza.com/ bruggebel>*. Centrally located, peaceful deluxe hotel. Well-equipped bedrooms, many with views of the historic Burg. In an intriguing blend of ancient and modern, the building incorporates the foundations of the demolished medieval St Donatian's Cathedral, part of the 10th-century city wall and a 16th-century cellar. 96 rooms, one of which is for disabled guests.

Dante €€ *Coupure 30, 8000 Bruges, tel: (050) 34 01 94; fax: (050) 34 35 39; <www.hoteldante.be>*. A quiet hotel situated on the banks of a canal approximately a ten-minute walk from the centre of Bruges. The atmosphere in this modern brick building is relaxed and friendly – staff are particularly helpful. The excellent vegetarian restaurant in the conservatory is open to non-residents *(see page 139)*. 22 rooms.

De Orangerie €€€ *Kartuizerinnenstraat 10, 8000 Bruges, tel: (050) 34 16 49; fax: (050) 33 30 16; <www.hotelorangerie. com>*. This luxurious hotel is wonderfully situated on the banks of the canal opposite Dijver. The staff are friendly, and the rooms are all individually furnished, with lavish marble bathrooms. Breakfast on the canalside verandah on a warm summer morning is a real delight. Guests can use the pool and sauna of De Tuilerieen, De Orangerie's sister hotel on the other bank of the canal. 19 rooms.

De Snippe €€€ *Nieuwe Gentweg 53, 8000 Bruges, tel: (050) 33 70 70; fax: (050) 33 76 62; e-mail: <de.snippe@flanderscoast.be> <www.grouptorus.com>.* This hotel oozes eighteenth-century elegance. All rooms are luxurious and many of them have impressive fireplaces. The restaurant, also called De Snippe, is one of Bruges' finest eating places. 9 rooms.

De Tuilerieen €€€ *Dijver 7, 8000 Bruges, tel: (050) 34 36 91; fax: (050) 34 04 00; <www.hoteltuilerieen.com>.* Sister hotel to De Orangerie, it is equally comfortable and friendly. The hotel is ideally situated just a few doors away from the main museums and with fine views of the Dijver canal from the front rooms. Pool, sauna, and solarium. Private parking lot. 45 rooms.

Die Swaene €€€ *Steenhouwersdijk 1, 8000 Bruges, tel: (050) 34 27 98; fax: (050) 33 66 74; <www.dieswaene-hotel.com>.* Lovely, romantic hotel with charming staff. The lounge was originally the Guild Hall of the Tailors. A separate wing, the Canal House, which opened in 2002, has 8 rooms, raising the hotel's total to its current 32.

Duc de Bourgogne €€ *Huidenvettersplein 12, 8000 Bruges, tel: (050) 33 20 38; fax: (050) 34 40 37; <www.ducdebourgogne.be>.* This small hotel occupies an attractive step-gabled house in historic Huidenvettersplein (Tanner's Square), right in the heart of the city. The hotel is elegantly, if a little over-ornately, decorated, with lots of tapestries adorning the walls and lavish antique furniture. 10 rooms.

Fevery € *Collaert Mansionstraat 3, 8000 Bruges, tel: (050) 33 12 69; fax: (050) 33 17 91; <www.hotelfevery.be>.* Small, friendly family-run hotel in an extremely quiet location just off Langerei, the long canal that reaches towards the north of the city. It has recently been enlarged and refurbished. 11 rooms.

Jan Brito €€ *Freren Fonteinstraat 1, 8000 Bruges, tel: (050) 33 06 01; fax: (050) 33 06 52; <www.janbrito.com>.* Beautifully restored 16th-century mansion, full of period detail, situated just a short walk from the city's major attractions. 18 rooms.

Montanus €€ *Nieuwe Gentweg 78, 8000 Bruges, tel: (050) 33 11 76; fax: (050) 34 09 38; <www.montanus.be>.* Tasteful, restrained elegance in a historic house, once the home of one of Belgium's most famous statesmen. In addition to the bedrooms inside the house, there are colonial-style pavilion rooms and a cedarwood honeymoon suite in the serene private garden. 20 rooms, one of which is suitable for disabled guests.

Prinsenhof €€ *Ontvangersstraat 9, 8000 Bruges, tel: (050) 34 26 90; fax: (050) 34 23 21; <www.prinsenhof.be>.* This elegant hotel is traditionally furnished, with wood panelling, chandeliers, and other antiques; it also has excellent bathrooms. There's a warm atmosphere, and the staff are very friendly. Possibly the best breakfast in Bruges. 16 rooms.

Relais Oud Huis Amsterdam €€€ *Spiegelrei 3, 8000 Bruges, tel: (050) 34 18 10; fax: (050) 33 88 91; <www.oha.be>.* This beautifully decorated, well-located hotel is a delightful, relaxing place to stay. The front rooms have lovely views over the Spiegelrei canal. 34 rooms.

Romantik Pandhotel €€€ *Pandreitje 16, 8000 Bruges, tel: (050) 34 06 66; fax: (050) 34 05 56; <www.pandhotel.com>.* A true gem in the heart of Bruges. Sumptuously and tastefully decorated, using items from the owner's antique shop. The Ralph Lauren Junior Suites are an idyllic choice for a honeymoon or romantic weekend. The excellent breakfasts are cooked on a cast-iron range in the breakfast room. 24 rooms.

Ter Brughe €€ *Oost-Gistelhof 2, 8000 Bruges, tel: (050) 34 03 24; fax: (050) 33 88 73; <www.hotelterbrughe.com>.* Extremely attractive hotel in the elegant St. Giles quarter, 5 minutes' walk from the centre of Bruges. Breakfast is served in the 14th-century beamed and vaulted cellar which was once a warehouse for goods brought along the canal. 24 rooms.

Walburg €€€ *Boomgaardstraat 13–15, 8000 Bruges, tel: (050) 34 94 14; fax: (050) 33 68 84; <www.hotels-belgium.com/brugge/wal*

burg>. Spacious, elegant hotel in fine, recently restored historic mansion just 100 m/yards from the Burg. All rooms have large, Italian marble bathrooms, and high ceilings and elaborate cornices abound. 13 rooms.

GHENT

Aparthotel Castelnou €€ *Kasteellaan 51, 9000 Ghent, tel: (09) 235 04 11; fax: (09) 235 04 04; <www.castelnou.be>.* Well presented apartment hotel in a good location near the historic city centre. Each apartment includes a separate bedroom, bathroom and kitchen/sitting/dining room, making it ideal for those looking to cater for themselves or for an economical choice if you are planning a longer stay. There is also an on-site restaurant and bar. Breakfast is included in the room price. 39 apartments.

Ascona €€ *Voskenslaan 105, 9000 Ghent; tel: (09) 221 27 56; fax: (09) 221 47 01; <www.ascona.be>.* A well-appointed, good-value hotel that is convenient for Sint-Pieters Station. 30 rooms.

Astoria €€ *Achilles Musschestraat 39, 9000 Ghent, tel: (09) 222 84 13; fax: (09) 220 47 87; <www.astoria.be>.* Although this is a very comfortable, convenient hotel, some of the rooms can be a little noisy, as the hotel adjoins the railway station. Disabled access. 18 rooms.

The Boatel €€ *Voorhoutkaai 29A, 9000 Ghent, tel: (09) 267 10 30; fax: (09) 267 10 39; <www.theboatel.com>.* A unique way to stay in Ghent – on board this floating hotel boat, moored on the river Lys, just 600 m/yards) from the main railway station. 7 rooms.

Chamade €€ *Blankenbergestraat 2, 9000 Ghent, tel: (09) 220 15 15; fax: (09) 221 97 66; <www.bestwestern.be/chamade>.* Modern yet cosy hotel, with good views of the city from the top floor breakfast room and bar. 36 rooms.

Charl's Inn €€ *Autoweg Zuid 4 9051 Ghent-Afsnee, tel: (09) 220 30 93; fax: (09) 221 26 19; e-mail: <hotel@charlsinn.be>.* Country house situated in private gardens 3 km (almost 2 miles) from the centre of Ghent and 1 km (⅔ mile) from the picturesque village of Sint-Martens-Latem, which was, and still is, a haunt of artists. Bicycles are provided for guests who wish to explore the countryside on two wheels. 9 rooms.

Flandria Centrum € *Barrestraat 3–7, 9000 Ghent, tel: (09) 223 06 26; fax: (09) 233 77 89; <www.flandria-centrum.be>.* Cheap, basic hotel in a quiet side street close to the cathedral. Ideal for those on a shoestring budget wishing only to sleep and wash there. Substantial breakfasts and friendly staff. No American Express or Diners Club. Some disabled access. 16 rooms.

Gravensteen €€ *Jan Breydelstraat 35, 9000 Ghent, tel: (09) 225 11 50; fax: (09) 225 18 50; <www.gravensteen.be>.* This 19th-century mansion, once the home of an industrial magnate, has been turned into one of the city's most elegant yet personable hotels. It is situated across the water from Gravensteen Castle, of which rooms at the front have a fine view, and it has been tastefully renovated and extended. Fitness room and sauna. Disabled access. 46 rooms.

Holiday Inn Gent €€ *Akkerhage 2, 9000 Ghent, tel: (09) 222 58 85; fax: (09) 220 12 22; e-mail: <hotel@holiday-inn-gentuz. com>; <www.holiday-inn.com/gentbel>.* Modern Holiday Inn conveniently located just a few minutes' drive from the city centre. Swimming pool, solarium, outdoor tennis court. Disabled access. 140 rooms.

Ibis Gent Centrum Kathedraal €€ *Limburgstraat 2, 9000 Ghent, tel: (09) 233 00 00; fax: (09) 233 10 00; <www.ibishotel. com>.* Cheerfully decorated modern hotel in an excellent location opposite the cathedral. The rooms at the front of the hotel have fine views of St Baafsplein, the cathedral and the Belfry. Some disabled access. 120 rooms.

Ibis Gent Centrum Opera €€ *Nederkouter 24–26, 9000 Ghent, tel: (09) 225 07 07; fax: (09) 223 59 07; <www.ibishotel.*

com>. A comfortable, modern hotel near the opera house and a sister hotel to the Ibis Gent Sint-Baafskathedraal. It's ideally situated for the medieval heart of Flanders. Other plus points include the extensive buffet breakfast and private parking facilities. 134 rooms.

Novotel Gent Centrum €€ *Goudenleeuwplein 5, 9000 Ghent, tel: (09) 224 22 30; fax: (09) 224 32 95; <www.novotel.com>.* One of the most attractive hotels in the Novotel chain, built around a central courtyard. The crypt incorporates 14th-century foundations. Facilities include a swimming pool. Some disabled access. 117 rooms.

Sint-Jorishof-Cour St Georges €€ *Botermarkt 2, 9000 Ghent, tel: (09) 224 24 24; fax: (09) 224 26 40; <www.courstgeorges. com>.* Most of the rooms at this hotel are actually in a modern, rather basic annexe situated across the road from the ancient building (originally the house used by the Guild of Crossbowmen), which dates back to 1228. The hotel's greatest asset is its highly regarded Flemish restaurant, which carries the same name *(see page 141).* Some disabled access. 36 rooms.

Sofitel Gent-Belfort €€€ *Hoogpoort 63, 9000 Ghent, tel: (09) 233 33 31; fax: (09) 233 11 02; <www.sofitel.be>.* Superbly located opposite the Stadhuis, the Sofitel Gent-Belfort offers excellent value for a hotel of this quality. The rooms are well appointed and extremely comfortable, with splendid bathrooms. Breakfasts are delicious and the staff are friendly and efficient. One of the two bars is in a historic crypt. Fitness room and sauna. Disabled access. 127 rooms.

Trianon I € *Sint-Denijslaan 203, 9000 Ghent, tel: (09) 221 39 44; fax: (09) 220 49 50; <www.hoteltrianon.be>.* About a five-minute tram ride from the city centre, this is a comfortable hotel for those on a tight budget. 18 rooms. A sister hotel, the Trianon II, Voskenlaan 34, tel: (09) 220 48 20; fax: (09) 220 49 50, has the added benefit of whirlpool baths.

Recommended Restaurants

There are so many places to eat in Bruges and Ghent that it is unlikely you will ever go hungry. Most cuisine is Flemish, which means in practice a menu heavy on seafood, but there are plenty of other choices available. Except for the most expensive establishments, it is rarely necessary to book ahead, although at the height of the season it is wise to arrive early to be sure of a table. Tourist menus and other set menus at a fixed price are very common and are the best value for money. It is also often cheaper to eat at lunchtime than in the evening.

Opening hours vary depending on the nature of the place. Cafés and bars are usually open for most of the day, as are many informal restaurants. Other restaurants will open for two or three hours to serve lunch, and then close until the evening. Prices are for a three-course meal including tax but not drinks. The restaurants listed here accept all major credit card unless otherwise stated.

€	below 20 euros
€€	20–40 euros
€€€	above 40 euros

BRUGES

Bourgoensche Cruyce €€€ *Wollestraat 41–43, tel: (050) 33 79 26.* Splendid gastronomic restaurant in the hotel of the same name. Eating out on the canalside terrace is a delight.

Breydel–De Coninck €€ *Breidelstraat 24, tel: (050) 33 9 746.* In the street that connects the Burg and the Markt, this long-standing proponent of the Belgian obsession with mussels has traditional style and wood-beam ceilings. It serves the mollusc in a variety of ways – the most popular of which is the basic big steaming potful – and all are worth going back for. Other seafood dishes, such as lobster and eels, have a place on the menu too.

De Belgede Boterham € *Kleine Sint-Amandsstraat 5, tel: (050) 34 91 31.* Friendly, small rustic whole-food café and pâtisserie. The menu includes fresh Flemish sandwiches and salads. Open daily until 5pm. No credit cards.

Den Braamberg €€€ *Pandreitje 11, tel: (050) 33 73 70.* Fine restaurant in a 17th-century patrician house just off Rozenhoedkaai. Modern, creative cuisine, with lobster a speciality. Closed Thursday and Sunday.

Den Dyver €€€ *Dijver 5, tel: (050) 33 60 69.* One of Bruges' finest restaurants, turning cooking into an art-form. Closed all day Wednesday, and Thursday afternoon.

Den Gouden Harynck €€€ *Groeninge 25, tel: (050) 33 76 37.* An exceptionally fine restaurant in a brick building that was once a fish shop (look out for the sign of the herring). If there is such a thing as Nouvelle Flemish Cuisine, then this is what they serve, and the wine list is superb.

De Karmeliet €€€ *Langestraat 19, tel: (050) 33 82 59.* Book well in advance to eat at this triple Michelin-starred restaurant, where chef Geert Van Hecke produces sumptuous French cuisine. Closed Sunday and Monday.

De Snippe €€€ *Nieuwe Gentweg 53, tel: (050) 33 70 70.* An elegant, Michelin-starred restaurant situated in one of the best hotels in Bruges and specialising in fish and game. Eating out on the terrace in fine weather is a delight. Closed Sunday, and Monday afternoon.

De Stove €€ *Kleine Sint-Amandsstraat 4, tel: (050) 33 78 35.* A small, simply decorated, intimate restaurant. Family-owned and operated, it specialises in Flemish dishes, with the stress on salads, fish and steaks. Closed Wednesday and Thursday.

Die Swaene €€€ *Steenhouwersdijk 1, tel: (050) 34 27 98.* French/Flemish cuisine is served amid elegant surroundings in the very fine hotel of the same name.

Het Dagelijks Brood € *Philipstockstraat 21, tel: (050) 33 60 50.* Fresh breads and cakes are on sale here, but go in for breakfast, lunch or tea and you should revel in the family atmosphere. Sit at the enormous central table that dominates the room. Closed Tuesday. No credit cards.

Huidevettershuis €€ *Huidenvettersplein 10, tel: (050) 33 95 06.* An elegant canal-side eatery (with an entrance on a handsome little square) specialising in Flemish cuisine. The building, which was formerly the Tanners' Guildhouse, dates from 1630. Closed Tuesday.

Kasteel Minnewater €€ *Minnewater 4, tel: (050) 33 42 54.* Charming, 19th-century chateau-style restaurant in a romantic location on the Minnewater. Visa only.

't Koffieboontje € *Hallestraat 4, tel: (050) 33 80 27.* Located in a hotel of the same name, this informal café-cum-restaurant situated just off the Markt is invariably crowded. The lively clientele is usually made up mostly of young backpackers, who are attracted by the extensive set menus, which offer excellent value for money.

Le Due Venezie €€ *Kleine Sint-Amandsstraat 2, tel: (050) 33 23 26.* This popular trattoria quickly fills up in the evenings, so arrive early to ensure a place. The vast menu offers everything Italian, including some good vegetarian options. Wheelchair access. Closed Tuesday. No American Express.

Maximiliaan Van Oostenrijk €€ *Wijngaardplein 17, tel: (050) 33 47 23.* Burgundian restaurant in one of the most romantic parts of the city, adjacent to the Begijnhof and the Minnewater. Specialities include the traditional local stew, *waterzooï*, grilled meats and seafood.

Patrick Devos 'Zilveren Pauw' €€€ *Zilverstraat 41, tel: (050) 33 55 66.* The 'Silver Peacock' is a lavishly appointed restaurant set in a 13th-century building, which serves as a showplace for chef/

owner Patrick Devos' stunning creations using fresh regional produce. Closed Sunday.

Spinola €€€ *Spinolarei 1, tel: (050) 34 17 85.* Romantic, beautifully furnished restaurant just off the picturesque Jan van Eyckplein. The food is in a class to match the surroundings, with fish a speciality. The extensive wine list features nearly 300 wines. Closed all day Sunday and Monday afternoon.

Toermalijn Restaurant €€ *Coupure 29A, tel: (050) 34 01 94.* A small vegetarian restaurant situated in the conservatory of the Alfa Dante hotel, serving organic food and wine. Closed Monday and Tuesday.

Tom Pouce €€ *Burg 17, tel: (050) 33 03 36.* This large but not impersonal restaurant enjoys an unrivalled position on the Burg. Although fish and Flemish cuisine dominate the menu, the quality of the food is definitely secondary to that of the location. Order a waffle or pancake, sit on the heated outdoor terrace and watch the world go by.

GHENT

Brasserie Pakhuis €€ *Schuurkenstraat 4, tel: (09) 223 55 55.* Pakhuis is a lively brasserie offering good modern Flemish and Franco-Italian cuisine. The setting – that of an attractively restored former warehouse – is especially impressive. Oyster and seafood platters are the speciality of the house. Closed Sunday.

Brasserie 't Klokhuys €€ *Corduwaniersstraat 65, tel: (09) 223 42 41.* Attractive brasserie set in an old building. Traditional dishes include Flemish stew and eel. Closed Monday morning.

Brooderie € *Jan Breydelstraat 8, tel: (09) 225 06 23.* Brooderie is an old-fashioned bakery selling excellent bread and cakes and serving healthy vegetarian lunches and snacks. Closed Monday. No credit cards.

Café Theatre €€ *Schouwburgstraat 5, tel: (09) 265 05 50.* Lively café-bar, popular with the younger crowd. Steak tartare is a speciality. Closed Saturday morning and from mid-July to mid-August.

Casa de Las Tapas €€ *Corduwanierstraat 41, tel: (09) 225 18 89.* This Spanish restaurant does a thriving trade (at lunchtime particularly) so it pays to arrive promptly. A friendly and lively establishment where you can chew in time to vibrant flamenco music. Closed Tuesday. Visa only.

Coeur d'Artichaut €€ *Onderbergen 6, tel: (09) 225 33 18.* A retro-brasserie serving succulent, beautifully presented and varied French cuisine at very reasonable prices. Closed Sunday, Monday and public holidays.

Eethuis Avalon € *Geldmunt 32, tel: (09) 224 37 24.* Vegetarian restaurant located close to Gravensteen Castle. Closed Sunday and public holidays. No credit cards.

Jan Breydel €€€ *Jan Breydelstraat 10, tel: (09) 225 62 87.* Overlooking the tiny Appelbrug Parkje and on the banks of the canal, the restaurant offers diners fine views as they enjoy their meals. Fish dominates the menu, often accompanied by champagne. Closed Monday morning and Sunday.

Keizershof €€ *Vrijdagmarkt 47, tel: (09) 223 44 66.* On Ghent's lively market square, this large, rambling restaurant has enough space that even when it's full it won't seem crowded. Diners pile into hearty portions of Belgian and continental food, amid a decor of wooden ceiling beams, plain wood tables and fashionably tattered walls. In summer, there's outdoor eating in the courtyard.

't Klaverblad €€€ *Corduwanierstraat 61, tel: (09) 225 61 74.* While most of the neighbouring restaurants try to lure you with music, 'themed cuisine' and moderate prices, 't Klaverblad is unashamedly gastronomic and expensive. French food is prepared with a Flemish twist. Definitely for serious eaters who appreciate good food. Closed Tuesday, Wednesday and Saturday morning. No American Express or Diners Club.

La Mal Contenta €€ *Haringsteeg 7–9, tel: (09) 224 18 01.* This Patershol-district restaurant serves one of the most specific of specialities – cuisine from the Canary Islands. This means plenty of fish, *paella*, *patatas arrugadas* (tiny skin-on new potatoes cooked in very salty water) and *mojo* sauce (made with olive oil, vinegar, garlic and coriander). Closed Monday and Tuesday. No American Express or Diners Club.

Panda €€ *Oudburg 38, tel: (09) 225 07 86.* Fish and vegetarian dishes served by friendly staff in a dining room curiously adorned in plastic and aquatic blues and greens. Closed Sunday. Visa only.

Patiron € *Sluizeken 30, tel: (09) 233 45 87.* A delightful café, where everything is made on the premises, including some hearty soups. The main speciality, however, is quiche, with over 80 delicious varieties to choose from. Superb vegetarian options available. The staff are friendly and helpful. No credit cards.

Sint-Jorishof-Cour St Georges €€€ *Botermarkt 2, tel: (09) 224 24 24.* An attractive and popular traditional Flemish restaurant in the historic surroundings of the Sint-Jorishof building, the city's oldest hotel. Comprising a single large room with a gallery at the front, the restaurant always seems to be doing a roaring trade. Closed Sunday evening.

Tête-à-Tête €€ *Jan Breydelstraat 32–34, tel: (09) 233 95 00.* This is an acclaimed French restaurant in a lovely old building. The food offered is inspired and the decoration stylish. Closed Monday and Tuesday morning.

Vier Tafels €€ *Plotersgracht 6, tel: (09) 225 05 25.* Located in one of the serpentine alleys of the Patershol district, this restaurant originally started with just four tables, hence its name. Now considerably enlarged, it has an ambitious and adventurous menu of dishes from around the world. Be warned: the spicy dishes really are spicy.

INDEX